Spy...
for nobody!

Sixteen years in the Syrian intelligence

Basel Saneeb

eKutub Publishing House
London 2020

Spy... for nobody!: Sixteen years in the Syrian intelligence
By: Basel Saneeb
All Rights Reserved to the author ©
Published by e-Kutub Ltd
Distribution: TheBookExhibition.com & Associates
All yields of sales are reserved to the author
ISBN: 9781780585420
First Edition
London, 2020

Contents

Introduction 5
Childhood and beginnings 7
A Treasure of Knowledge and Education 19
    My role in establishing a secret organization against Assad regime 29
My first success 55
The Gruesome Period of the Academic Studying 65
    The shocking surprise and the hard-fateful decision! 87
    The years of working in the Military Intelligence Branch in Hama 93
Finally, The Tyrant died... 141
The difficult years 147
Two years in the army 165
The detention 171
The second defection 183
Epilogue 189

Introduction

I begin my book and story with asking for blessing through mentioning the name of my true, one and great God/Allah, the most merciful for everyone and at all times, and Praise be to Allah, Lord of universe, May the blessings and peace of Allah be upon the most honored of messengers our master Muhammad and upon all his family, companion and followers. Then:

This is my biography and my personal life. I decided to put them in this book, although, I'm not an expert in the field of authorship, literature or writing. but I think and - Allah knows best - that my experience and what I have been through and had done in my life, especially my work in the Syrian military intelligence department\intelligence service, for almost twenty years, contain enough weirdness, uniqueness, danger, excitement and benefit for the reader, and attracts him to follow up, with emphasis for who is going to read, all those events, personalities, and places to be mentioned are true and from the reality as I explained it, with respect to misrepresentation of some names just to preserve the privacy of those people and their safety. Any event or detail mentioned in this biography, I can - god willing - prove its authenticity and accuracy and by witness testimony from people who have lived and participated and witnessed these events, and most of them are still alive as of the date of this writing. I also had various official documents, from various sources, confirming all information I had written. I used to collect and keep them lifelong at my home. Unfortunately, all these documents were burned and destroyed with my house, which was looted and bombed and burned by the

Syrian regime in the 3rd month of 2012, one year after the Syrian revolution.

  I ask god to help me and guide me with his generosity for my work to be useful, and to have his satisfaction.

Childhood and beginnings

The important events, which changed the course of my life, started in February 1982.

I was born in in 1975, in Homs, a city in the middle of Syria. It forms with its countryside the largest province in Syria in terms of administrative area; and is characterized by the kindness of its people and its beautiful climate. The river Al-Asi passes next to the city and grants it more beauty and magic. In short words, Homs is a distinctive city in everything; and all Syrians know this. May no humor be told in almost all of Syria, without mentioning the people of the Homs city as a role in it.

My family is a Muslim family on the Sunni Doctrine, which was with "average income". My father was a government employee in the wheat mills in our city, Homs; and my mother was house wife and taking care of us, despite the fact that her education at that time allowed her to get a teaching job in a primary school; but my father - may God have mercy on him - as the habits and dignity of the people in the city of Homs at that time, wanted to be the sole breadwinner of his family, despite the difficulty of living expenses year after year, because salaries - that were given to employees in the 1980s by the governments of the regime of Hafez al-Assad - were very few compared to expensive prices and life hardship. Most of the foods and consumer goods were very scarce in the country, as a result of what was called "the years of the economic siege on Syria," knowing that I am certain that the majority of the Syrian people never dared to ask about this siege, who imposed it !? and why!? because the question in my country Syria was meaning often death or imprisonment and torture until death!

I was the middle son of this family, we are three brothers, males only.

Of course, I had to give you this brief overview of my upbringing and family, because this will inevitably help you to understand many of the details of events later.

We return here to 1980s, specifically February 1982, when I was seven years old. But why I chose this exact period to start the story?

Of course, any Syrian reader or anyone interested in Syrian or Arab affaires will probably have known the answer already directly, because at this date, the Hafez al-Assad regime did massacres in Syria, a lot of massacres that are not similar to almost any other ones in the past and present history. The most severe one at that time is the massacre of the syrian city Hama, when they destroyed the center of it almost completely by burning, bombing, and the demolition of houses over its inhabitants, without interruption for a whole one month all that was done by the forces of al Assad polity. Many of the inhabitants of this city were slaughtered, abducted and tortured, and large number of their daughters were raped. The inhabitants who survived after all of that, were arrested and tortured terribly. The criminals of al-Assad polity cut the limbs of many of them, they continued to do that until the victim's death. Many people in Hama were arrested by al-Assad forces and brought to prisons, and never appeared after that, and there isn't any information about them whether they are alive or dead, and how and when they died!!

These massacres were later called "the events of 1982, the events of Hama, or the events of muslim brotherhood"

The reader here may think that I diverged or moved away from the main story; but this is not true, because my strange life story was almost related to these events and their effects.

Now, the reader has to know, without going into the many, many details of these events and massacres, which alone need volumes to explain them, that what was happening in brief (which are facts that the Syrian people understood later on over the years) appeared on the surface that the Hafez Assad regime was eliminating a hostile party or organization to him and his regime, which is the Muslim Brotherhood (Ekhwan Muslemeen). But the truth was much deeper and further than that. What was going on was pre-planned by the Nusayri/Alawite community in Syria and whoever supported them globally, such as the Communists, Zionism, and the Iranian Magi regime.

This scheme was agreed upon for a long time, and its details are that the Al-Assad Al-Ba'ath Nusayri regime (a religious minority whose percentage in Syria at that time does not exceed about 2% of Syrian people at the best estimate. They were living in rural mountain regions inside underdeveloped and barbaric communities before the Assad regime's occupation of the country. /The English Writer and missionary Samuel Lyde after living for six years in their villages talked about them in two books -The Anseyreeh and Ismaeleeh: A Visit to the Secret Sects of Northern Syria with a View to the Establishment of Schools (1853) and The Asian Mystery Illustrated in the History, Religion and Present State of the Ansaireeh or Nusairis of Syria (1860)-, about how their community was a "perfect hell upon earth", as he described it) rules Syria. In fact, this regime was subjugating and enslaving the Sunni Muslim people, who make up about 80% of the Syrian population, at the least estimate, through religious sectarian elimination for all personages of the Sunni people, including scholars, clerics, students, scientific researchers, academics, politicians, officers, and everyone who may poses any current or future threat to the regime. He was seeking to get rid of all those who could think of any political ambition or claim the right of this Sunni Muslim majority to make sense of the rule and sovereignty of their country.

The only way available for Hafez al-Assad's regime to achieve this scheme was bloodshed, with bloods of Sunni Muslims going to be the terrifying firewall that would enable this regime to remain in power for almost fifty years afterwards.

Many non-Syrian readers may not know that the largest and most well-known massacres were in the city of Hama. However, it affected almost all other Syrian cities. Assassinations, massacres and arbitrary arrests affected all the Syrian cities in particular, and some rural areas. The massacres and arrests were particularly systematic towards the elite men and youth of the Sunni Muslim majority everywhere, and of these places, of course, is my city Homs.

My early childhood was a normal childhood. However, since February 1982, despite my young age, I have noticed a change in everything and everybody around me. I do not know whether it was an early awareness that God had made for me to prepare me for what will happen next or is it something that others of my generation also had!?

Since that month of that year, I began noticing a change in the faces of all persons around me. Laughter and even smiles were beginning to decrease in the faces of adults. I began to hear conversations, sometimes whispering and sometimes faint conversations, even if they were happening in closed houses and places, about what happened in the city of Hama, and about the killing, kidnapping, and assassination of people every day in the rest of Syria. The random arrests were everywhere, and the charges were always ready for everyone, and they are often "affiliation with the Muslim Brotherhood (Ikhwan Muslemeen) traitorous gang" as it was called and marketed by Hafez al-Assad regime to be called at that time.

I always heard about names of people I knew, including my father's relatives. I also remember one of our neighbors, a man from a well-known family in Homs. I still remember that he used to give me sweets whenever I saw him, and he had a huge library indicates to his vast culture. That man has disappeared after his brutal arrest by the Assad regime forces, and no one has ever seen him again thereafter.

Warnings were addressed to us, as young children, everyday; such as: "if anybody asks you or tries to make conversation with you about Nusayris, don't answer him and always say "I don't know anything about that". Moreover, if your teacher or anybody else asks you about Hafez Alassad, always answer: we love Mr. President very much!"

Generally, I felt that fear was widespread everywhere around me, at school, at home, in the bus, and in the street. People, in my Sunni community, used to speak whisperingly and with obvious fear reactions on their faces so that they were looking around continuously when they were speaking about these topics wherever they were even in their houses!

Indeed, it is very strange, isn't it? Definitely, Syrians who lived in that time know what I'm talking about very well, and certainly know the very common proverb then: "Walls have ears".

Despite of all of that, almost all adults were not careful to that extent when I or any age-matched children were present. As they considered us not aware enough to these topics yet.

Shortly after the Hama Massacre, a remarkable event happened in my city, Homs. In that time, all houses in all Sunni's neighborhoods were being roughly and violently inspected by the intelligence and military forces of Assad Regime. I still remember that day when I woke up in the morning and heard my parents talking about how soldiers and intelligence forces members came to our house while I and my siblings were sleeping. They invaded our house and inspected it thoroughly, as they did with all other houses, without any consideration to houses' sanctity or people's privacy. Of course, there was no justification for that, furthermore, they did not even have any inspection warrant. That was very common as Assad regime put the country under the status of Martial Laws, which is similar to the emergency status implemented by states in wars. In such status, everything become permissible for the state, so that the persecution, injustice and violation of people's freedoms become normal and even legal!

Although I was very young at that time, this event made me angry and annoyed and woke up myself and family defense instinct. This was not only a violation of laws of all human communities in the world, but also a violation of our customs, traditions, and religion which guarantee the sanctity and privacy for women. It is not accepted at all that strangers invade houses, without any convincing reason or justification, and mess with the furniture and clothes, especially which belong to females; and no one dare to object or to say even a word.

In that time, because of all these events and people's comments about them, I started to hear and recognize the most dangerous, prevalent, and intimidating word for Syrian citizens, since the early infiltration of Hafez Alassad and his sect "Nusayris" into the rule centers until the emerging of the spark of the Syrian Revolution, that word was "Intelligence= Mukhabarat (as Syrians name it)" which is the name of the Sectarian persecution intelligence systems that have been established by Hafez Alassad. These evil forces took various identities and different names, but almost all their members were Nusayris. Furthermore, Hafez Alassad used these armed forces as assault and oppression tools against the innocent Syrian people for more than 50 years. Paradoxically, I became an officer in one of these intelligence systems for almost 18 years; actually, I did have my own reasons which I will narrate with all its details later.

After that period, I noticed that all people in our Syrian Sunni community live their daily life with "Intentional Schizophrenia". Even us, as children, were also supposed to live in such status as the elders always commanded us. They were repeatedly warning us from the terrible consequences for us and for our families in case we forget or refuse to become schizophrenics. It was indeed a strange collective phenomenon, how? And why we must be schizophrenics?

Schizophrenia is a mental illness in which the patient imagine that he has another personality accompanying him, or there is another soul in his body, he adopts with that by living as two different individuals. Unfortunately, that was the only lifeline for Syrian Muslim Sunni people to survive and avoid the oppression of the most sectarian and criminal regime.

In secret, everybody hated Hafez Al-assad and his Baathist-Nussayri regime, and they considered him as a human devil, but no one dare to express that. Actually, the expression of these thoughts and attitudes in anyway, either by words, movements, reactions, or even by facial expressions will mean a deadly end not just for the person but also for his family, his relatives, and sometimes his friends, in case the regime's spies notice that. This was not a science fiction or unjustified fear, it was fact and reality; the syrians heard such news almost daily all over the country.

As a result of all mentioned above, it was inevitably required from us, as Sunni people, to live with two different personalities every day for all lifelong. In all situations, we were demanded to show love and loyalty for the Assad regime, and continuously express our respect to his portraits and statues which were spread in every street and every square in Syria.

Indeed, his portraits were printed on the front page of all scholar books and pads even those for Kindergarten's pupils. The images were actually in every street and bridge, as well as on all walls and corners of the governmental and military buildings. This was not arbitrary, this was according to the regime's belief that Hafez Al-assad is the number one doctor, teacher, wiseman, farmer, and worker. They believe that Hafez Al-assad's behaviors, words, and opinions are all extraordinary; they teach them for young and adults, in schools and universities as core subjects included in exams. Everyone disobeying, or even just thinking of disobedience, will be undoubtedly sentenced to death.

While stories about the Hafez's regime injustice and oppression were daily trending among relatives and families behind the locked doors; these stories were always followed by curses upon him and wishes to see his end. The speakers were always looking around with afraid eyes when they told such stories; they were always cautious that someone hear them and take them to unknown lethal fate no one knows, except God, where and how this fate will be.

One of the strangest things that may be mentioned about the uniqueness and awful abnormality of the Syrian situation, is that the Assad's regime is, according to my knowledges and readings throughout my life, the most repressive and oppressive regime all over the world. It is well known that all oppressive regimes, including the Nusayri regime, may arrest people randomly, fabricate charges for them, torment them, or even execute them, as well as their families or anyone who may have any relation with them. The Assad regime outperformed all his pairs in criminal practices so that it was forbidden in Syria to ask about or to track news of any political detainee whatever your relationship was, even if it was your parent, sons, daughters, wife or husband. It is really the most shocking, strange, and sad thing in the universe.

Not just that, but furthermore, you are, according to the Assad regime, not allowed to ask about who arrested your relative (after you saw him being kidnapped in a brutal way), where he is detained, or whether he is dead or alive. It was prohibited to ask about detainees regardless how long their detention period has lasted, and anyone infringing this will be vulnerable to either severe threat with some hours of torture or they will fabricate a charge for him, if he was unlucky, and face the same fate of his detainee.

It pleases me to mention a beautiful, honorable, and heroic attitude by my father, may God rest his soul, few people dared to do like it in that time. That is, after the Hama Massacre, which I mentioned earlier, the regime and his intelligence services asked from all members of the Arab Socialist Baath Party, whose name contains a huge amount of lies and deception, to carry arms and to participate in persecuting and oppressing people.

Unfortunately, Sunni Muslims consisted a big proportion of the members of this party in its early beginnings although it was like other regime tools directed to consolidate the rule and to oppress the people. There were two main reasons which pushed Sunnis to enroll in this party: the first one, is as many of them were deluded by the idealistic, sonorous and nationalist slogans raised by this party. Those, including my father, God rest his soul, thought they had done the right thing, and did their national duty to build the future of their country, and they did not feel the trick and trap that the Assad regime had set up until the emerge of the sectarian racism nature of this party and other organs of the Assad regime during and after the Hama Massacre in 1982. The second reason is regarding to the Syrian generations that came after this period, including me and my relatives, friends, and neighbors, we all were mandatory joining the party. As the enrollment to this party became later a kind of a ritual of compulsory allegiance to the regime. If you are not a member in AlBaath party, your procedures in schools and universities will be harder, you will also suffer during your military mandatory service, and you will not be able to get a governmental job, knowing that the job in government departments at that time was almost the only available source of income to the most middle-income Syrians.

My father was an ancient member of Alba'ath party, which meant that he was eligible, if he wants, to take up an important position in the future. Despite that, he strongly refused the regime's commands of carrying the arms in the faces of his country's citizens. This refusal, like any other anti-regime acts, perhaps meant in that time a lethal end for my father and for the entire of his family as well, but he insisted on this refusal so that he was pressured and threatened, then he was referred to a partisan court and he was dismissed from the party. My father has miraculously survived as God protected and saved him from death. It was a severe experience, my father and everyone who know this story still told it proudly, of course in secret and only for trustful people, because it has become a testimony of honor and high morality of my father. Thanks to Allah, the God of the worlds.

A Treasure of Knowledge and Education

In this period and while my childhood years were passing under the above-mentioned circumstances, as God will, we had got new neighbors in 1984, whom had a strong remarkable influence on the events of my life later. Thus, it is quite meaningful to speak about this family and their influence which will be mentioned more often throughout talking about the upcoming events.

This family which moved to live in our accommodation, in a flat above ours, consists of three persons: father, mother, and their only son. The father, Abu-Iyad, was an officer with intermediate military rank in the Syrian army, this rank was quite enough to frightened people since the Syrian people used to fell scary from anything related to government or military. The mother, Om-Iyad, was a teacher in elementary school, but because of her husband's position and influence, she became the director of this school later. Iyad was the name of that son, who was corrupted by the flattery and being spoiled from people around him and his family, because of the avidity and personal ambitions which all people around him were seeking for through the influence of his parents. His parents, in their role, made Iyad used to get everything he wants no matter how expensive or difficult it was, they never said no for anything he asked for. Not just that, but also there was a torrent of gifts and bribes that were poured on him from every side of the acquaintances, relatives and neighbors, most of which was a dream that was difficult to achieve for any other child of our time. The reader, who does not know the details of the Syrian situation, may wonder why all this!!? What is the importance of just an ordinary officer in the army so that he and his family can enjoy advantages that even some ministers in other countries may not enjoy!?

Here I must go back again to explain the specificity of the relationship between the Syrian citizens and the State that was led by Assad criminals. It is well known that in all countries, the army officer, out of his working hours, is an ordinary individual in the community, and doesn't have any privileges more than others; however, in Syria there is a different situation, where the intelligence or military officer remains like a sword directed to the necks of people, especially because of the massacres, persecution and repressive rule that was depending on intelligence control that have accompanied the Assad regime's abandonment of Sunni Muslims in most state sectors by demobilizing them from the work, at best situations, or by fabricating any charges against them and arresting them, particularly in the Syrian armed forces where that was happening in an intensive manner. In that time, most of the officers and noncommissioned officers in the army, and police leaders belonging to the Sunni majority had been eliminated and replaced by others from the Nusayri minority. In the intelligence services, the substitution was almost complete, with some rare exceptions of those who have proven their loyalty and blind obedience to the Assad regime, and baptized this proof by blood shedding of innocents.

Achieving this purpose, the youth from the Nussayri minority were recruited in the Syrian Armed Forces quickly and daily, throughout the rule of the criminal Assad family, which lasted for more than 45 years. As results, Nussayris became the dominant and the strongest part of the Syrian Armed Forces, in almost all state's bodies and sectors, and even in the civilian government, which was civilian just in its name but in fact it was military administered. This malicious strategy centralized power in the hands of this sect's individuals so that no one dare to face them or oppose, as the only armed force was under their control. This was actually the strangest and most dangerous task that Assad and his sect could success to achieve in their path to rule Syria. Therefore, Syria became, as I know, such a state that differ from all other countries in the world. For example, in all world states, soldiers, intelligence members, and governmental employees are a mix from all population ingredients, therefore, part of them will support the people demands in case if any protests or demonstrations happened, because they are a part of this population and maybe their families, relatives, and neighbors are involved in these actions. While as in Syria, the army, the intelligence, and all armed forces became all a racial entity that is isolated and differ from other population. Nonetheless, how to such an isolated and spiteful group to sympathize or align with the Syrian people, this is impossible as most of this population are Sunni, who are the traditional and eternal enemy according to the Nussayri sect's holy books, beliefs and legacies

As a result of all mentioned previously, the power and the influence of the army on the civilians, and on the civil life aspects, were very strong and different from any other state, because it derived from the fear of the people from anything that is related to the government and rulers, moreover, the power, prerogatives, and influence of the intelligence services' officers and workers were much more than their peers in the army. More in-depth details will be given later, if God will.

As mentioned earlier, some people from Sunni areas have proved their absolute loyalty to the criminals, therefore, Assad regime appointed them in non-basic positions along with some power and formal privileges as well, and allowed them to be involved in some armed forces of his regime, nonetheless, this was limited, thoughtful, and definitely under monitoring. Doing so, the Assad regime achieved many crucial and important goals which helped him to still dominate on the people all these years. These goals, in my opinion, were:

- Dispersing the unity of Sunni Community, and instilling disputes and hatred among its members; you can imagine if someone, who was harmed or even lost one of his family by the regime, sees that some of his people and community's members are working with that regime; absolutely this will grow up the hatred.
- Penetration: it is well known that all repressive regimes rely on the acquisition and recruitment of traitors through which they can penetrate the ranks and know the secrets of any society or group.
- Deny the charge of sectarianism and racism and improve the image of the regime in front of the world and Arab public opinion: where Assad regime was and still talking as a normal popular rule, and not that racial sectarian repression rule, by showing and highlighting some Sunni officials in front of the world and Arab public opinion. Whereas, those officials, as I explained before, and as I knew and was confirmed through my work in intelligence services and through my life, all were nothing but an imaginary façade, and have no real opinion or decision in the state

policy, and their authority was only over their own people for the reasons and purposes that I mentioned earlier.

Daraa province and Al-Rastan area in the countryside of Homs were the most important Sunni regions that their inhabitants had been allowed to have such exceptions, as all Syrians know. So that some officers and officials from these regions didn't just showed no objections against Hama Massacre 1982 and the events before and after it, but furthermore they participated with Assad regime in these crimes, therefore, they were rewarded by allowing to some of them to be in some limited powerful positions at Assad regime.

Our neighbor, Abu Iyad, was one of this type of officers who were overlooked by the Assad regime. He descended from Bosra area in the countryside of Daraa province. Because of what I explained previously, his military rank and position had a big influence on his life as well as his family's life and everyone around him. While as, under Assad regime rule and for many years, it was enough to any officer to wear his uniform with his military ranks so that most things would be simple and easy wherever he went in Syria. For example, he could employ any one in a governmental job, could move an employee to another job, could move a student from school to another, could use his relationships to exempt a merchant from a financial penalty which he as an example got from the Consumer Protection Department, could provide a family visit permit to an imprisoner, or could support any solider during his mandatory military services in a way that could help or change the fate of that solider throughout this service which may last for 2.5 years or more.

In addition to that, there are many things which could be done by any officer, military employee, or intelligence employee. All these dirty jobs pass through a complex system of bribery. These bribes which were called by the corrupted Assad regime as gifts and tips, were daily transmitted among all Syrian community members, that society which was completely vitiated by Hafez Assad's rule.

Because of all above, if any citizen refuses any request or order from any officer, in this case that officer can simply make the life of that citizen to be very difficult, even more, he can simply fabricate any political charge for that citizen, and put him in prison maybe forever.

Due to all that, our neighbor, officer Abu Iyad, and his family enjoyed what we and all neighbors and relative around us couldn't have the same. For example, having a car was an unachievable dream for almost all middle-income Syrian citizens, while as Abu Iyad had two cars, one was owned, and the other given to him by the army. Gifts were poured on him, his wife, and his son daily and with large amounts; nonetheless, people were racing to please them wherever they existed. After they moved to live in our building, and because of my mother's convergence and friendship with Om Iyad, and because Iyad was the same age as my elder brother, so they became classmates in the school, I started to visit them along with my mother and my brother.

Iyad, who is the only child of this family, was a selfish, arrogant, "narcissistic" person as a result of many reasons, some because of his family as he was their only son, and other because of those people who treated him well to gain his father's satisfaction. In addition to that, he used to be in the center of the interests of everyone around him, and they didn't refuse any request from him; therefore, Iyad had what could be described as the Palace of Dreams or the City of Wonderland for any ordinary child of an ordinary family, like me at that time.

Since my first visit to Iyad's room, my amazement and astonishment were very strong. Just because a little boy had his own room was something that most people around me couldn't get, so how if this room was full of toys and scientific tools which were too expensive and imported from abroad? For instance, that video player which was newly known in Syria in that time, and many rich people couldn't have; in addition to many things that were a dream for children and adults as well. However, the happiest and the most important surprise for me was that huge and amazing collection of books, stories, world novels, folders, and encyclopedias, which were at the top of my interests and played a big role in my life. For me, that library in that time worthed more than any Gold treasure in the world, so that I was still sticking to these books and this family for about six years by all what the word sticking means. During these years, I endured the severe rudeness of Abu Iyad against me and how he more often expelled me from his house. I endured also the arrogance and the bad mood of Iyad as well as his constant attempt to exploit me against my elder brother, who was Iyad's rival classmate, for that reason, Iyad was continuously conspiring against my brother in order to surpass him in study and everything. Furthermore, I endured my family criticism and their astonishment about how could I accept all this rude treatment from Abu Iyad's family, and still insist to be sticking to this family and visit them every day and all the time. However, I didn't concern about all of that, all what I was doing is diving in the seas of books, reading, science, and education, so that my family nicknamed me "books' worm" because I was reading the books which I borrow from Iyad everywhere and all time, even during meals or when I enter the bathroom.

How often did I spend many nights awake! because I was reading a world novel, a scientific article, a philosophic essay, or a history book, so that I go to school next day without sleeping. I did not refuse or leave any kind of science and books, even those that others would reject or regard as strange or that they only concern those who are specialized in certain fields of science, or that they do not fit my age such as psychoanalysis, philosophy or political and military books. Not even one day passed without borrowing a new collection of books or folders from Iyad. The nice thing is that God Almighty has facilitated to me this renewable and unlimited treasure of books and science, because as far as I read and finish from these books, the father of Iyad was bringing more and more of them, as gifts from people as what we mentioned earlier; most of these books were rare and expensive and not available for many people.

The most preferred types of books for me were the historical and documentary ones, which I was reading with extreme curiosity and passion as if I would be examined, especially those talking about intelligence services and the experiments of global spies who worked for the various agencies and countries in the world. I read about their successes and failures, how they work, how they behave and act, and what are their goals. Consequently, what I studied, memorized and understood at the time of that type of books became part of my personality throughout my life, as I will mention later!

This period of very intensive reading has had a profound, beneficial and very significant impact on my future, my culture, my thoughts and my knowledge of global ideas, experiments and experiences. Praise, and great and endless Thanks be to Allah, the God of all worlds.

My role in establishing a secret organization against Assad regime
that aims to step down the regime and get rid of its impacts

Years were passing quickly while I was immersed in reading, as I mentioned in the previous chapter, besides that, my father, God rest his soul, was keen to teach me all time the good thoughts which we must learn about Islam, such as the equity for oppressed, not to oppress people, and not to prejudice others' rights, the satisfaction with God's sustenance, looking for Halal livelihood, and many other honorable and well known Islamic teaches. Unfortunately, all these teaches were completely in contrast with what was common in Syria in that period, whereas Assad regime was spreading the corruption, bribery, and immorality so that people began to consider that things as normal. Under the rule of Assad regime, the most dangerous and lethal charge for the Syrian citizen was to pray in mosques, and attend the religious lessons by the scholar of religion in house or in mosques, furthermore, to have a beard, which is a personal freedom for everybody, was a suspicion and charge which may put the person under intelligence monitoring by regime's spies and agents, with a high likelihood of being arrested or even executed. Therefore, almost all parents were always asserting on their sons to comply with the daily precepts, such as:

- It is preferred to pray in the house; we know that the pray in the mosque is a duty and its reward is more than praying elsewhere, but we don't want to draw the attention of the regime in order to avoid problems.

- Avoid carrying on religious conversations in public, except with those who you fully trust.

And many other things which were increasing the ambivalence and schizophrenia in our life. I was always linking, in my mind, between teaches of Islam that my father taught me and what I had read in books about the heroes from various nationalities who sacrificed their life to rescue their people and support their ideologies or to eliminate the injustice, arbitrariness, and occupation in their countries. Because of that, and despite my early youthfulness at that time, my confidential constant obsession was the question of:

- What can I do for the oppressed people of my nation, their case and situation?

- Will I live afraid and oppressed all my life like how my father's generation lived?

- Is this corresponding to my humanitarian and Islamic dignity?

God willing, when I became 16-year-old, in the secondary school stage, I met a group of youths matching my age then, during one of summer school camps which were imposed by the Assad regime on all Syrian students in attempt to instill its envenomed thoughts and its criminal ideologies in the minds of the students from their early youthfulness; like the hallowing and sanctification of Hafez Al Assad, and other things which are in complete contrast to and oppose all the thoughts, legacy and traditions of Syrian Muslim Sunni People.

This group of youths became my best friends later, we became colleagues and partners in thoughts and in life during the period that followed the camps, especially because we were from the same origin, we were brought up with similar education, religion, social background, and personal and domestic suffering from the injustice of Assad regime; consequently, we became a closely interconnection group very quickly.

Among this new group, a young man called Ahmad was the most eminent member, the closer to my method of thinking, and the most similar one to me in the personal education level that was different in our peers. Ahmad was member of a middle-income family, like most families in our society, his father, God rest his soul, was working in food trading, in addition to his work as a muezzin in a mosque in our city Homs. They descended from a damascene family, but they settled in Homs long years ago. Because of his father's job as a muezzin, Ahmad had the opportunity to obtain more scientific and religious culture than his peers; by attending educational lessons, reading books, and interacting and interchanging knowledge with disciples who, by God's grace, did not stop attending religious lessons in the mosques of Homs despite the huge amounts of oppression against them by Assad regime

As a result, to these circumstances, Ahmad recognized closely, or even lived in the status of injustice, compulsion, and humiliation which were directed against all whom or what is related to Islam and Sunnis in particular. Although these practices were directed against all people, they were concentrated severely and intensively toward all who work or study in the Muslim Sunni religious fields, like as orators and muezzins of the mosques and the owner of religious libraries. Ahmad saw, many times and many days, how his father and his friends were arrested or periodically recalled to the intelligence branches; therefore, Ahmad became increasingly aware and responsible, and started to ask himself the same questions that I asked myself before: What can we do?! How could we save our families, people, and beloveds from this constant tragedy?!

Actually, since our first meeting at the camp that I mentioned previously, each of us felt that he found the partner whom he was looking for whereas, both of us used to feel himself stranger among his peers before we met each other. It is normal for those who are 16-year-old, our age in that time, to have pretty normal interests that every peer had, such as making friendship with girls, playing, sports, and other things that would make up the most of their behavior and conversations. Therefore, everyone who has more serious or deeper interests than these subjects, like me and Ahmad, will definitely feel himself as stranger among age-matched peers, and will find vast differences between the cultural, political, historical, and religious conversations, which are the center of interest for me and for Ahmad, and the quality and the content of the topics that others are interested in.

Before knowing each other, we were both compelled to establish friendships with elder persons, perhaps we found among of them someone who has the same interests and narrations. As a result to all above, and since our first meetings, I and Ahmad were like a thirsty person who finds water suddenly after a long time of thirst, thus, we stayed, for many years later, completely companioning each other all time and everywhere at school, at home, in cold and hot weather and in all circumstances; so that we had never been satiated or sufficient from exchanging information, discussions, thoughts, projects, dreams, and planning for future. We had never been separated unless for eating or sleeping, then quickly joined together to complete the argument that we opened before, to explain a book, or to talk about an experience.

An absolute confidence was generated and firmly established between us since the beginning of our friendship very quickly and in a short time; despite the rarity and gravity of this matter among Syrians at that time. Almost all our narrations and discussions were automatically, sometimes intended and sometimes unconsciously, directed toward the political situation and the tragedy that we all lived under the repressive and dictatorial rule of Hafez Al-Assad the criminal and his cronies. Considering that just to be a friend of or to meet with someone who, or one of his relatives, has any relation with mosques and religiously adherent persons, is an extremely scared matter to any Syrian citizen; as he knows that this relationship will put him and his family under the microscope of the Assad regime's intelligence men; therefore, my family were afraid about me and about themselves as they knew about my friendship with Ahmad, and tried more often with all ways to end this relations so that they used violence with me as well as with Ahmad sometimes; particularly, when they knew that we meet in the mosque, and we attend the sermons and the religious lessons in mosques or at some homes constantly and secretly. These events increased my anger at the general situation in Syria, as well as my assertion to maintain Ahmad's friendship; because I believed that I do the right thing and I chose a good person to be my friend, furthermore, I knew that all people including my parents believe that he is a good friend too. In normal situation, my parents should be happy and proud of their son as he is committed to the good morality, attendance the mosques with his friend, and the various scientific and religious narrations instead of wasting his time, like other guys, with playing and learning bad habits like being Alcoholic, watching porno movies, or do other bad things which were common among youths.

But unfortunately, the deviant social and political situation, which was established by Assad's sectarian regime during his rule of Syria, made the corruption, the immorality, and the debauchery acceptable and secure, nonetheless, this regime encouraged these behaviors and spread them among the Syrian People in order to weaken and to scutter the minds of these people to force them to stay under his dominance, and to prevent the existence of people like me and Ahmad who think to eliminate this regime and its injustice; of course, because this will be dangerous for them and will threaten the regime's existence. In addition to that, the dutifulness, the commitment of Islam, and the unlimited thinking were made by the regime to look like frightful things, so that people became scared. Due to all previous reasons and details, I excused my parents and appreciate their attitude and behavior "God forgive them", they were the same as about 16 million Sunni Muslims who were all oppressed in Syria.

As a result to my parent's fear, in addition to the length of our meetings which made us in need of a place where we don't annoy our families by sitting in it for long periods of time, we began to meet privately at a garden in front of Ahmad's house, in order to not disturb anybody; we kept meeting, discussing and sharing everything between us for more than fifteen years on the same seat of that garden. Sometimes, the rest of our friends in the group would join us, so that our families, neighbors, the parkgoers and all those who knew us would know that we are constantly sitting in this park.

We were always sitting on that seat of this park for long hours and everyday despite of the hotness in summer and the severe cold and snows in winter; so that all who saw us were very astonished from this behavior. We chose that seat particularly because it was a safe place as it was in the middle of a public park and nothing there could obscure vision, therefore, none of the Assad intelligence agents and spies, who were everywhere, could draw near us without feeling them and being aware of, furthermore, we were sure that no one can guess that we are talking in such dangerous and anti-regime conversations with that simplicity and in public park while nobody dare to do that even in closed secure places. Indeed, this thinking and planning was successful for a very long time.

In that place, we discussed, talked in various topics, and performed so dangerous things that any of these things was enough to fully decimate us, our families, and the families of our friends as well, in case one of the Assad regime's partisans knew that. In fact, many people, sometimes along with their families, were executed by this regime because of less important and dangerous speech than what we were discussing in at that place; The funny thing is that we called this seat where we meet in the garden cynically and jokingly "Conference Palace".

In fact, the extreme courage, and the youth eagerness, as well as the reformist goal of our Syrian society, which was our dream and soul hope, were the reasons behind acceptance to put ourselves and our families within this horrible danger for long years although we were just young guys whom no one may believe that we can endanger or threat anybody.

The same question was repeatedly being asked between Ahmad and me, that is, what can we do according to our weak possibilities to save or even to participate in rescuing our society from oppression

We had studied, reviewed, asked, and learned, for many years, about all what we had heard of the experiences of parties, regulations, and revolutions in Arabic states and the whole world to know the factors of success and failure; we did our best to increase our information in this field. For example, if we have heard about a prohibited book by Assad regime since its author was one of the debaters of Muslim brotherhood party or any restricted party else, and we knew where that book was, then we were still planning and working insistently until knowing the owner of the book and getting it and then reading it. Moreover, if we have heard that someone was released from the prison after being arrested by the Syrian oppressive intelligence service, we would do our best to meet him and gain his trust in order to listen to his experience with Syrian intelligence systems and how they work. Upon every success in such missions and after every new information, the discussions between me and Ahmad, and our trust zone friends, were igniting and might last over days and maybe months; about how could we mimic the methodology of the parties and movements which we learnt about; unfortunately, almost all these discussions always reach to dead end due to the extreme barriers which have been established by Assad regime for monitoring and stopping any similar political, revolutionary, and intellectual activity against it, in addition to the complete control that was applied on all the people everywhere, nonetheless, our competencies which were almost zero, particularly fiscally, as we were still students getting our pocket money from our parents.

These behaviors continued to be repeated between me and Ahmad for three years, until we became at the end of high school stage when our self-confidence became higher and higher, at that time, we realized that the time of speech and discussion is over and now is the time for actions, thus, we took the decision which has a great impact on my whole personal life later. The action we decided to do and did it at that time was such a serious plan that no one dare to implement it in Syria no matter how much brave he was, furthermore, those who dared to do "like the Muslim Brotherhood" faced their deadly fate. We have decided to establish an organization against the Assad regime in order to become a core for a larger political party, if Allah Almighty helped us in that. Actually, our plan was to start by inviting all of our trusted friends and classmates to join this organization, this, of course, would be done after they pass the final confidence tests, These tests were carried out by Ahmad and me with agreement and coordination among us without letting the targeted person feel that he is being examined and tested at first, thereupon, we invite them one by one, depending on all what we have read and learnt about the experiences of global intelligence services and memos of spies, that Ahmad and I have been passionately reading and studying for years. To do that, we used to give the targeted person some secrets and imaginary tasks that carry just a limited risk on us, thereafter, we wait and observe his reaction for a while, in case everything goes well, we try to know indirectly to what extent his level of enthusiasm is for the idea of liberating our Syrian people from the Assad regime, and what is the degree of his readiness to enroll, take the risk and sacrifice for this goal; by mean of discussions and conversations with him, when we agree that he is ready and appropriate for our organization, one of us invites this person individually, personally, secretly, and directly to join this organization, and then absorb his reactions, which are often intense horror and confusion at first. We were interested in monitoring and studying these reactions later in order to get benefits from their results to improve our method of inviting; that was always being done along with our readiness to answer appropriately about some intuitive questions that most people will ask upon inviting them, examples of these questions are:

- Will we be affiliated to any other known organization or party?
- The answer: no, we are just a group of young people who want to obey Allah the Almighty, and do our duty towards our religion, our homeland and our society as well, by attempting to remove injustice far away.
- • What should we do, and what is required of those who accept to join?
- • **The answer:** presently, the only thing required is your approval of the idea and the principle, and to increase the number through nominating other new members whom you think that they accept to join us, they must be trustful. As usual, these new candidates will be monitored and tested long enough before inviting them to join the organization, of course, this must be done under the condition of maintaining the absolute secrecy and adequate camouflage, moreover, without showing any tendencies towards this kind of ideas and actions in public.
- • Do we have any resources of funding?

- • **The answer:** right now, we consider ourselves as a simple core with humble potentials as being students, however, we will research to funding resources if Allah helps us, maybe by bringing in people who have financial capacity and who are already convinced and have the desire to fund this matter that serves the issues of their people, or by collecting contributions from the organization's members in case that the number becomes sufficient for self-funding.

And other questions that vary by people.

Our success has been good and semi-complete regarding to those who are from the close circle of friends around us, because we had already chosen them previously and were still in friendship with them, and because some of their ideas and tendencies converged with our principles. Almost all approved, and they joined us despite the fear and panic that appeared on their faces when we directly suggested them joining us; sometimes Ahmad and I, In good faith, were enjoying once seeing their reactions and observing the emotions on their faces, then we discuss these reactions and the questions they asked to benefit from the results while we invite others later.

The success, represented by the number of associates, was good for beginners like us, especially with our very modest potentials, Ahmad and I stopped for a short time when discussing the suggested name for this organization, whereas, we were restoring in our minds the names of Arab and international organizations that we know or have heard of, perhaps we use it to name our nascent organization, however, Ahmad suggested something which I accepted because it is practical and simple, his suggestion was that no need to be hurry in accredit a final name for our organization until the number becomes larger, and the self-confidence as well as the inter-confidence increases among its members; consequently, this will also reduce risks if the Assad regime arrests one of the members "Allah forbid", Ahmad suggested to choose a false and ridiculous name, that doesn't arouse the attention or seem to be dangerous so that only those who are from our group will know what it means, and it be a coded name between us, we have called it "Group to teach young children to enter the bathroom", we laughed and ridiculed a lot at that name, and we laugh every time we tell someone who is with us in the organization, although it was a simple idea, it seemed to me at the time as an innovative genius idea, it enabled us to talk about any topics related to our organization even if we had to talk about it in a public place without drawing the attention of anyone.

In this period, Allah guided me to success in the high school and getting its certification. As a result of my constant research and thinking about what is the next possible step in the way toward our goals, an idea has emerged in my brain, about what we will do after creating an organization and recruiting members, what is the first step that we will be able to take against the Assad regime? Thereupon, I had many ideas to answer these questions, for example: Are we going to distribute leaflets inciting people to revolution and rebellion? Will we write phrases against the regime on the walls? Will we attempt to get weapons if we find funding resources and train our organization members for the armed resistance like most revolutionary organizations in the world?

Here, the next fact came to my mind: Who is our greatest, most dangerous, and the most frightening enemy? The answer: of course, the intelligence services and security forces of the regime that are widely extended in Syria, so what is the best way to beat them or confront and challenge them!? The answer: we never have enough information about them, because the Syrian intelligence system was formed mostly from officers belonging to the ruling Nusayri sect, which is a sectarian minority that sanctifies Hafez al-Assad, It is almost impossible to penetrate them by recruiting one of them, because their full benefit is in remaining faithful for their regime, i.e. the Assad regime.

So, what is the solution? How will we encounter our greatest fears and our biggest enemies?

At this point of thinking, at that time and after I got my high school certification, I was at the stage that I and every student should choose his specialty and in which university, academy or field he likes to study, so a clear, dangerous and bold idea came to my mind!

Why don't I try to penetrate this terrible intelligence system?

Why do I not seek to work inside it and become an officer in it?

Is there anything better and more successful to any oppositional organization, in any country in the world, than having one of the members who is even the founder working as a spy within the most important and sensitive device of that regime, which the latter fully depends on in keeping its power and control over the people!?

When my mind arrived to this solution and to this result, I immediately felt that the beats of my heart accelerated so that it would nearly explode, and my stomach began cramping, despite that ,thanks to Allah Almighty, I have never been afraid of any creature, but this plan, if it successes, might be the best plan in the world, on the other hand, it might be the most stupid plan that leads to a terrible perdition if it will not be done well, or failed or was exposed, moreover, the likelihood of success or failure is not known, only Allah Almighty knows that. I am also a young man and I was supposed to start establishing my future, and to enjoy the normal life at the university, as all my peers will do, perhaps with this plan I will have sacrificed my future and my life, and threw myself into a terrier of demons and criminals who do not resemble me or I resemble them in anything, but I will have to live and work with them until the end of my life or for a time only Allah Almighty knows, and I should accept that despite them being enemies of me and of my people, this is all for a purpose, only Allah Almighty knows whether I can achieve it or not !!

My next step was presenting this idea and my plan to my partner and friend Ahmad, to know his opinion on this and to discuss with him its details. I can confirm that I am until the moment I am writing these lines, and although twenty years have passed since that moment, but I still remember and can't forget Ahmad's reaction when I asked him for an urgent and very confidential meeting, then I came to his house and we were alone there because his family had left the house, at the moment that I finished explaining my idea to him, his eyes popped and he flickered as if he had been bitten, and I felt that the wall of absolute trust, which we have built through years of friendship, brotherhood and partnership, almost collapsed at this moment, whereas the instinct of fear and suspicion of treachery and betrayal overcame him, these behaviors that the Assad regime planted among the people for decades, by recruiting traitors and agents, some of them agreed to betray even their family and relatives, the first phrase that Ahmad said was: " If you really do that and will be employed in any kind of the Syrian Intelligence services, at that moment, consider that I don't know you and have never known you all my life, and I won't know you anymore".

However, after very long discussions about what my plan is, and how I do not intend to only be a spy for our organization within the Assad intelligence, but also, I planned, if the plan succeeds and I become able to cheat them well, in addition to the usual acts of spies that I intended to implement inside the intelligence service system like sabotage, leaking information, and planting rumors and disorder among our enemies ... etc., I will try to be helpful and supportive, and mediate for others from the Sunni community to employment and work in this system, and plant more and more persons like me inside it until we can slowly enter into the organs of the regime, and increase our number among them, similar to what they did with our people previously so that we will reflect the magic on the magician, because the members of the Assad Nusayri sect once in the past infiltrated and took the control of the army, intelligence, and the armed forces gradually, in the same secret way at first, until they managed to seize Syria and its people later although they are a small minority.

Ahmad knew just like me, and as I explained to him, that if this plan succeeded, it would have a great impact on our struggle against the oppression of Hafez Assad's regime against our people; but the biggest, most important and most serious question is: will a young man like me succeed in this work and breakthrough that an entire population has been unable to do!? how long will the enemies need to discover me and execute me!?

Here, I must point out something that most Syrians may know, while others don't know about, that is a bad anomalous characteristic that distinguished the Assad regime in Syria from any other regime, it is that when someone becomes an employee, worker or officer in the Syrian intelligence services in any status or military rank, he can never leave this work and get out of it when he wants, unless he has a permanent disability, mental illness, great psychiatric illness, or of course the death, this means that it is an irreversible path! I wish Allah helps us in this.

It took some time until my friend Ahmad became convinced despite his justified doubt in the proportions of successes and failures in this plan, thereafter, an another necessary and difficult phase began, where I must inform my parents about the subject and convince them by this idea, this must be done without explaining to them the real reasons and motivations that I will do this for "because they didn't know anything about our secret political organization", that I haven't told them anything about, insuring their own safety, as well as the safety and the secrecy of the organization."

This task was not easy at all, it was almost impossible that my parents accept the idea that I, their young child who they raised on morals, and they think he is committed to the teachings of Islam religion and to avoid causing harm to any human being, despite all this, now I want to join and work with the dirtiest and most dangerous criminal gang in the country, those who killed, displaced and assaulted hundreds of thousands of Syrians, and they oppressed an entire population counting millions!

It was a very difficult mission to convince my parents, it took months, Allah has inspired me a plan to convince them by doing different kinds of problems with them, being absent from the house for too long time, and declining to register at any university or institute to complete my studies after I got my high school certification, until my family reached a conviction that I became a mindless young man, and I am almost wasting my future, and I was walking in the path of corrupted young men who have no good future. However, when they arrived into this stage of despair of my situation, I told them that I wanted to enroll and work in the Syrian intelligence service, of course, they were amazed and categorically rejected, furthermore, they scoffed at this idea at first, but, due to my insisting and repeating of this idea over and over again, as a single solution, that provides me a job and assure my future "As I explained to them that this is the only reason", my parents began to accept the idea reluctantly, or maybe they thought it would be a fancy or a reckless idea put forward by their mindless child who is unaware of the consequences of thing, so they agreed to the idea temporarily.

While I was attempting to persuade them, my father "I ask Allah to have mercy upon him and reward him with all the best" was offering me alternative solutions according to his humble possibilities to assure my future, he told me once if you wanted me to help you, I will rent a store to work in any profession you choose, and other times he told me if you want to complete your studies in any field, I'll pay for it as much as you want, but I always faced him by my insistence more and more on my thoughts. When they both noticed that there was no escape from approving my decision, they asked me a realistic and surprising question, because, in the midst of past events, I forgot to find an answer and resolve it, the question is: If we agree with you that you will be employed at the Syrian intelligence service, who will help you to achieve this goal !?

Their question was, no doubt, correct, since the intelligence systems were so sectarian that no one could be employed without mediation, sponsorship and support from an officer of the same system, or one of the officials from within the government and the state. Certainly, the entry of a young Sunni Muslim, who is committed to his religion and is from a family with an anti-Assad background, and employing him in the intelligence services It was very difficult.

I felt that first of all I had to beg Allah by supplication. Yes, I must pray and ask my God/Allah to guide me and protect me, because despite that I persuaded everyone around me but there are still some doubts in my heart about the validity of my decision and my plan, therefore, I started the prayer for getting Guidance from Allah and said:

O Allah my God, if you know that this matter is good, satisfy you, and it make me closer to your path, help me and make it easy for me, and if it is evil, keep me away from it, or show me a sign of its evil.

After my prayer, and because of the grace of Allah - Almighty -, and because he wants me to complete my destiny, I saw in my dream white clouds, I considered it a sign from Allah Almighty that my plan will be good, and really after that, the things became easier what made me think is proof of my sincerity in this matter, and Allah is the greatest and he knows best.

After deep thinking and prolonged searching about a way that I can enroll in an intelligence service, I remembered a group of people whom we know in our society, they are among such a few people who have good relations with some officers and officials of the Assad regime, thereupon, I decided to ask my father to try talking to them one after another until we find someone who can help me reaching my goal. Due to my extreme insistence on him, my father made his first attempt with one of our acquaintances, he is Abu Tariq, although he was one of the hypocrites and sycophants of the Assad regime and his organs and associates, but he refused to help us in this matter, his pretext was that if any young Sunni Muslim like me employed in any intelligence system, it would be like suicide, and he showed his disapproval of the whole idea. Here, I remembered our neighbor, officer Abu Iyad, the officer that I talked to you about him and his family earlier, however, when my parents talked to him about my desire to be employed in intelligence services, and asked him to help me with this, he disapproved strongly at first , furthermore, he was amazed like anyone else, but after my parents explained the situation to him, that I did not leave to them any solution to guarantee my future he agreed hardly and reluctantly, and he affirmed that he completely disowns the consequences of this matter, and he holds me the responsibility for any outcome!

According to God's Will, Abu Iyad was working in a highly training and educational military academy in this period, as a lecturer, teacher, and trainer for senior regime officers, who work in all intelligence, army and armed forces services, and they all were in need for him and wanted to please him, and ready for providing any service to him, in order to gain his support to success and pass this military training. When Abu Iyad agreed to help me to enter one of the Syrian intelligence services by finding an officer from the Nusayri sect, the ruling Assad sect, Abu Iyad's approval did not only assure that I will become an officer in one of the intelligence services, moreover, he asked me to choose any kind I want from the Syrian intelligence services, because he has officers from all that different services whom he can make them help me.

Therefore, I immediately started quick researching, in addition to what I know before about the types of intelligence and intelligence services that exist in Syria, and what are the differences between them, we, as citizens, knew that there were different kinds of these services, but because they are all harmful to people, no one really cared about the difference between them, however, I need to know more about the differences between them now, in order to choose the right service precisely and correctly that would be more useful for our secret organization.

There were many intelligence services in Syria, but the most dangerous administrations which the system was depending on to support his rule, control the people, and monitor them, were four kinds namely:

1- Military Intelligence Administration "Military Security Forces" or "Al-Mukhabarat Al-Harbia": It was assumed according to the meaning of its name and its specialty to be responsible for monitoring and tracking the intelligence affairs of military and armed forces, their workers, officers and employees, but it was the largest intelligence service in Syria in terms of number, equipment and support. In fact, it was the most sectarian administration which caused much harm to people, the system was fully dependent on it even in the control of other intelligence services and all the civil and military sectors of the state. Moreover, the heads and leaders of other intelligence services were often selected from among the officers of this administration.

2- Political Intelligence Administration: It is supposed to specialize in political affairs, intelligence of police force, and internal intelligence, but like the other ones, it intervened in most citizens' affairs.

3- State intelligence Department " or the General Intelligence Department": its officers in Syria are less than other devices, and it intervenes in everything like others.

4- Airforce Intelligence Department: At first it was just like its name suggests specializing in monitoring the air forces, air defense, and officer pilots, Then, it became like others intervening in everything.

Forthwith, I chose the Military Intelligence, because it is the strongest, the most influential, and powerful, and it is the closest to the decision-makers in the Assad regime. Here, I remember a funny thing, when I informed officer Abu Iyad of my choice of military intelligence, he was more surprised and angry, and he said to me: Not only you want to be employed in the intelligence of the regime, but you chose the worst and harshest of them, too, where Sunni Muslims are fewer than in any other one among its employees, they are almost nonexistent in this administration, and as usual I answered him by increasing my insistence on my thoughts and choice, which made him yell angry and disowned from me and from the results of my actions, after he will finish helping me, stressing that he is doing this in order not to disturb my family from him only.

Then, as usual the care of Allah Almighty surrounded me, thanks to Him, shortly after I talked to Abu Iyad, he summoned me to his office at one of the military educational academies in the Syrian capital Damascus, and summoned another colonel working in the Military Intelligence administration, he introduced me to him, and asked him to help me to volunteer as a non-commissioned officer in that administration, although my high school diploma allowed me to volunteer as a regular army officer, but my goal was precisely the intelligence system. For me to become an officer with higher rankings in it, the only way in Syria was to volunteer first in the army, then after long and varied courses, and great mediations I can become so, but, no one can guarantee that I can move from the army to the intelligence, it was possible that I won't move, then my efforts and sacrifices are in vain. So, I chose the safest and fastest route, which is accepting to be employed as non-commissioned officer that means with lower military ranking, but this was the surest and fastest way.

For the intelligence colonel, it was too easy to do, he sent me directly in one of his luxury cars with black glass to the first intelligence branch that I entered in my life, it is the leading branch of the Military Intelligence administration, its symbolic name is the branch / 291 /. Something funny happened to me when I entered that branch is that, while the car was taking me to the intelligence branch and the driver is also an intelligence agent, my heart was beating fast because of excitement, when we arrived at the too tight intelligence zone in the center of Damascus, the guards of the gate and entrances opened the huge gate and started to make the military salutes like they usually do for the senior officers, however, they did that because they did not know who is in the car as its glass was totally blinded so that it was difficult to recognize who is actually in the car. This matter made me laugh and gave me another evidence that Allah Almighty takes care of me and protect me.

Thereafter, the driver accompanied me through the branch to the recruitment office, which is called voluntary office, as it is usually being called in intelligence, military, and police sectors in Syria to distinguish the volunteers (those who join willingly) from the officers, non-commissioned officers, and professional individuals who are performing the compulsory military service that all Syrian citizens must complete, those individuals are called compulsory soldiers.

I met, in that recruitment office, a noncommissioned officer named Abo Hasan. He was the chief of that office, and of course he belongs to the Nusayri sect. He took comprehensive and extensive details about me, my personality, about my family, my address, and all the information and details he could get about my life, then, he asked me to write all this information within forms. As will happen with everyone I will meet throughout the next 18 years, which I have spent among them in the Syrian Intelligence Services, this man could not hide his surprise from my affiliation to the Sunni Muslim majority, as well as my wish to be recruited and working in the intelligence branch! in addition to that, I am from the city and not from the countryside either. This second reason always was more surprising for him and for others hereafter, because rare few of Sunni Muslims which remained recruiting in some of the Assad's intelligence services, were always and exclusively from some rural areas, as I explained previously. because the Assad regime used a new and despicable planned conspiracy after the Massacre of Hama (1982), that plan was to stir up hatred in rural areas -that were at that time isolated and simple- against the cities' residents, and he planted this hatred through education methods and mass media, against the urban people in Syria, he focused on planting ideas in the minds of some of these simple rural people, for example that the people of the cities belong to the "feudal and bourgeois classes", that they were and still "hating and deriding all the rural areas people and getting disgusted from them", and enslaved and exploited the rural people formerly, and took their ration with injustice and aggression. Therefore, they said and lied that the Assad regime, his sect, and the Alba'ath Arab Socialist Party (which is a party that the Assad regime uses as a political interface, and the most of its members come from countryside Syria), came to save the peasants and the countryside people from all this injustice and seek justice for them.

By spreading these convictions, this regime could sow the seeds of the hatred and antagonism, and then the cleavage between members of the united Sunni community. Furthermore, they marginalized and excluded the people of the main cities of Syria by making the preference always for the countryside people while accepting the applicants for governmental, civil, and military jobs throughout the Assad period. Therefore, the number of workers who belonged to these cities became much less than before in the civil sector of state functions, and almost extinct from the military sector, and became zero in the intelligence functions, for more than forty-five years of Assad's father rule and after him his son Bashar the atrocious.

The army sector was almost empty of urban Sunni Muslim people, in addition to their totally absence from the intelligence services, especially in the military intelligence branch because it was a completely sectarian entity .I was, thanks to God, for sixteen years - a lot of people know this - the only Sunni Muslim urban employee who works in this entity, for this reason Abu Hassan the chief of recruitment office- was surprised, and maybe annoyed, but he could not appear any opposition or obstruction against my registration and admission, because of his fear from the colonel who sent me to him with his driver and ordered him to support me.

After the interview in the recruitment office, another appointment was determined weeks later, where I have to come to the branch to make an exam and oral interview with a committee of Senior Officers and the founders of the military intelligence administration, after my examination this committee will determine to accept me to work for them or not.

When I finally got out of the branch in that day, I thanked God and praised him so much, because what I have completed on this day was the first step in a long and prickly way to my plan and my goal, which I prepared for a long time in my life before.

My first success

in penetrating one of the dirtiest Intelligence Services systems in the world, and the most powerful in criminality, ferocious and isolated one

After a short while, when I was recalled, I undergone a group of medical and military tests (they are usually conducted for all candidates of military and intelligence jobs), I have successfully passed them all with God's help. But during that, I noticed how much the diffusion of corruption, nepotism, and the bribes was prevalent among the officers and the officials of the Assad regime, and among individuals of Nusayri sect itself. During the medical examinations, there were a lot of the young men, who were refused by doctors because they are medically ineligible, or with a dysfunction in their bodies, but they returned soon accompanied with one of their relatives who are officers or officials, to mediate for them with the doctors, and soon the results would be changed, so that they pass the medical examination and be accepted to work in the intelligence forces !.

In late 1993, It was the time for the fateful interview with a committee of senior officers of the Military Intelligence administration, in order to screen and test candidates for working in this Intelligence system, whereas they determine the validity and personality strength of these candidates, this test was usually called ((psychological examination)), on the day of the interview, I had a cold and a very strong flu, in addition to my normal high tension because I will go to the den of criminals and cutthroats of the regime, furthermore, I will meet the enemies of me and of my people there, I will be exposed to their checking and questions, this is never easy certainly.

During my travel from my city Homs to the Syrian capital Damascus, then crossing the streets of the capital towards the main branch of the military Intelligence administration, I was very dizzy, nauseant, and vomiting all the time so that I emptied everything in my stomach all the way.

When I arrived, that branch was crowded with young candidates like me, as I remember the number was about 600 candidates, they all gathered in the middle square of the branch. Some of them were in the crowd at the door of the test room, they were all, as I knew, from the Nusayri sect, we, as Syrians, distinguish them from their own dialect in speaking which does not resemble any other dialect in Syria.

I have been waiting for them for many hours to call out my name to enter the Committee, but I noticed that the situation is bad, and the method of determining who enters this test is similar to what I saw earlier in the medical examination, I mean corruptions and mediators.

After I got tired of waiting, I felt an increased severity of my sickness, also, I started to worry after I noticed that the examining committee may not meet all those candidates, and they might just be satisfied with the people they met until now, and the others would be refused, - If this happens- the efforts and planning I and those around me previously got tired for, will go in vain. At that moment, God inspired me to an idea that I decided to implement immediately. I entered the office of one of the branch officers without permission, indeed this behavior was risky, however, this officer is the one whose office I entered once on my previous visit to this branch, when he was told about my wish, when I was sent to by intelligence colonel to apply for this job.

I told him quickly, and I ignored his surprising and angry looks from my courage and rudeness of how I enter the office, that the colonel who sent me earlier asked me to tell you that "you must intervene immediately with the examining committee to enter the examination quickly because I am sick".

Actually, my plan was so effective that the officer called someone by phone for few seconds then he told me to go back and wait at the door of the committee room because they will recall me soon; however he did that without being sure whether I was honest or not, maybe he wanted me to go out his office as quickly as possible to go back to his work.

Indeed, after few minutes I heard someone calling my name, finally, I entered and stood in front of a committee of the Syrian Assad Intelligence Service Administration, it was composed of senior officers, just the name of any one of them is enough to scare any Syrian citizen at that time, because anyone of them can simply, and without any exaggeration, end the life or disturb the future of any Syrian by one order, all the Syrians who lived at that time know very well the accuracy of what I say.

The Chief of this committee was a Nusayri officer at the rank of colonel named /Ali Ziwanah/, he is a senior veteran officer in this work, and one of the founders of this bloody intelligence service. When I saw his face, I immediately realized that he is a cunning and evil man. Since I entered, he and the other members of the committee started examining me with their eyesight from my head down to my feet, at the same time they were reading my data and full information about me in the files that were placed in front of them, then I immediately noticed on their faces what I expected, it was the same surprise that I noticed earlier on the face of all intelligence officials when they knew my desire to work with them, whenever they knew that I am a Muslim from the Sunni majority, and from the city, and I intend to join the intelligence, for these reasons, I was a strange and striking phenomenon that is different from all others, so that I still had been watching, all my life and my work in the Intelligence Branch, then in the army, an amazement on the face of any new person who knows about me.

And then, committee chief started asking me simple normal questions about my life, my family, and my studies. However, because of my travel and my severe illness, in addition to the extreme hunger I felt because I didn't eat any food all the day and I emptied my stomach due to my illness, above all, I was very nervous and waiting in the branch square in a cold weather for long hours before entering to the committee, all this made me feel very dizzy when I was standing in front of them, furthermore, during answering their questions, I was no longer able to feel with my arms and legs so that I expected to fall on the ground in front of them at any moment, and to lose my consciousness. I was struggling hard, my thoughts focused on reminding myself that it is unacceptable to lose everything because of a minor illness after all what I did and sacrificed with, and what my parents suffered from to deliver me to this moment.

I asked myself, is it possible that a simple flu can eliminate my plans and efforts?!

At that moment, Allah Almighty gave me the courage, I asked, in quick successive sentences, permission from the Chief of the committee to speak, then I explained to him that I am very sick and I feel dizzy, and how I shouldn't leave the house today and receive the necessary medical care, but I came despite all this in order not to miss the exam, it appeared on the faces of the members of the committee that they were convinced of what I explained to them, so that they allowed me to sit considering my health, unlike other candidates who should stay standing during the interview. Whereas ordinary persons in Syria are prohibited from sitting in the presence of intelligence officers unless there is a special permission from them. After that colonel Ali the Chief of the committee ordered someone to bring a glass of water to me. At this moment and because of this water glass, the interview wholly and suddenly changed, so how did this happen?

It is known to most Syrians that the Nusayri sect, Al Assad sect, are alcoholics, they even sanctify Alcohol in their religious books and satanic beliefs, unlike the Sunni Muslim majority whose their religion and beliefs forbids drinking any kind of alcohol, The most common type of alcohol among the Nusayri sect is a very alcoholic drink they call it " Arak ", and all of them manufacture it manually in their houses at the time of grape's maturity every year, they have special tools for that, they usually manufacture large quantities enough for a year, they take pride between each other in the quality, taste and intensity of effect of what each house has produced from this intoxicant. This drink has a transparent appearance and is without color, but it becomes white almost like milk if it is mixed with water or ice.

When I was in the interview, and they brought to me a glass of water and I hold it, I noticed that the color of the liquid in it was white and not as the known transparent water color, I knew later that the water in Damascus is always like this color because it is mixed with chlorine and because of its extreme pressure, but I didn't know that before as I didn't live in Damascus. So, when I saw this color, I became afraid and expected that it could be a trap or kind of test done by this intelligence committee to make me drink the arak until I lose my balance - Allah forbid - because they knew that I am from the Sunni majority who are not used to drink alcohol.

For that, when I hold the glass, I hesitated to drink it for a moment until I smelled it first to make sure its water, by the habit and because of my severe fatigue, I forgot my caution for a second and I moved my lips with the name of Allah without a voice (like all the Muslims do before they eat or drink) and I drank, all this happened in quick moments, unfortunately, it was enough to the expert, malicious and trained eyes of the intelligence committee officers to take notice of it, I felt that the matter became very dangerous, they were clearly finding that I am certainly not the type who would normally want to work in the Syrian intelligence service, and one of his main tasks was to combat the spread of Islam and religion, observing and persecuting religious people, and keep people away from all that binds them to their religion, how does someone like me come and wants to join them!?

Uncertainty, suspicion and surprise became apparent at the Chief and the members of the committee. After I sat down and drank water, I regained some of my composure and consciousness, thereafter, I felt that I would need everything

I studied, read, and trained myself on in the previous years from the experiences of spies and intelligence men in the world to avoid the effect of the scenario of the cup which provoked doubt in the hearts of the committee members, otherwise, everything will be lost, and maybe me too.

Immediately, and in way that colonel Ali, the committee Chief, thought it was abruptly, but I expected it and was ready for it, thanks to Allah, he asked me a question:

- Don't you drink alcohol?! he said it while looking carefully at my face!
- I replied with deliberate calm: of course not! his astonishment increased because of my daring in declaration my disapproval and my opposition which challenge all their beliefs.
- He asked: why don't you drink it?
- In this moment, I realized that my answers must be completely deceived and evasive, and I must avoid any answer that refers to the religiosity, therefore, I replied quickly: for me, I have a strong conviction that I must refuse and hate anything that makes my mind fail or stop working even for a moment, then I looked into his eyes and felt that I had answered well.
- He asked me: do you pray?
- I told him: Yes of course, all the officers looked at each other and to me surprisingly, their features and gazes became as if they saw a space alien in front of them, their appearance was saying what is happening here! and what is someone like this doing here!?
- He asked me: do you usually go to mosques?

- I answered: Yes, I go with my father to mosques every Friday for the usual congregational prayer.
- He asked me: if you wanted to get married in the future will you choose your bride from those who wear the hijab?
- I replied: Yes of course.
- He asked: do you have relatives detained for membership of the Muslim brotherhood? during the Assad era if this is proven to be true of anyone, this certainly means his rejection in any ordinary government job, so how if it was a sensitive intelligence job.
- I replied: No.
- He said, after looking at the information about me which was in my file which was in front of him: your answer is incorrect! here it is said that one of your family is a political detainee because of his relationship with the Muslim brotherhood!
- I said to him: we are a very big family in Homs, and our number is large, for that, we don't all know each other, city life is not like rural life, the great distances between the streets, and so many people make the acquaintance even between family members difficult, and we hardly know some relatives of the family

In this moment and for the first time during this interview, one member of the committee spoke, his name is Hanna, Christian officer, whose rank (2nd Lieutenant) was the lowest among the committee officers. He told me angrily and wrathfully: are you crazy?! I said to him with a smile showing my self-confidence to minimize as much as possible from their surprise from me, and from my answers: you are asking me axiomatic questions, its answers must already be known to you, therefore, I replied frankly and honestly because I have nothing wrong or must be afraid of or need to hide, so I don't need to lie and give you incorrect answers in order to satisfy you.

- He said: how is this!?

I said to him: all you asked me about were traditions, customs and heritage that exist in my community and everyone does it to keep up with those around him, it is not related to any opinion or direction of thought or anything else, I am just an ordinary person like others, I am matching and following the habits around me. By this answer, I intended to look stupid, and put in their mind that I am just a simple Youngman who imitates without thinking, and follows the habits of others in blindly way, I excluded of myself the characters of comprehension and the religious tendencies that it is impossible for them to be agreed with, because they see any thought different from theirs as the greatest threat to their existence and their continued rule in Syria.

Then, quickly and in a way that the Colonel, the Chief of the committee, thought it was surprising to me, but he didn't know that I expected it and I was training and preparing myself for such things long time ago, he asked me a question:

- What do you think about religious fundamentalism? this name was circulating at that time as a result of the emergence of religious movements which caused controversy in Egypt and Algeria, because It was opposed to the repressive dictatorships regimes there, and in the media, they called them fundamentalists. I replied quickly, confidently and without hesitation: my opinion is exactly the same as that of the grand leader, Mr. President of the republic, I intentionally revered and exaggerated him as followers of the regime love to do, Hafez al-Assad, who answered an anchorwoman of an American news agency when she asked him that same question, this answer is:............. Then I mentioned to him the whole answer that their boss had said literally and without missing any word, even though that answer was long, and even though the meeting with Hafez al-Assad was very recent, only a few days ago, and it was shown on television only once, of course there was no internet in Syria at that time. Once I finished, Colonel Ali the Chief of the committee stood up, he could not hide his pleasure and admiration as if I had read to him a piece of a holy book, he told me with enthusiasm: you are excellent you can go you have passed the examination!

I finally got out of the room, in which I stayed double the time which all other candidates spent in it, as I stepped outside I was thanking God and praising him and repeated to myself: Allah is great Allah is great, I felt that the hand of care from God continues to help me. What had happened in this place was my first success in penetrating this regime and the intelligence branch, and my intellectual victory over these criminals. Me as a young man with humble capabilities succeeded for the first time in my life in cheating a committee consisting of the elite criminal minds, and manipulated the minds of those who succeeded in humiliating and subjugating millions of Syrian citizens and stole a whole country, praise be to Allah, thank you God all the time and forever

The Gruesome Period of the Academic Studying and the Military Training of the Intelligence Service

The reputation of security and intelligence training courses has always been famous and terrifying, it is known in all countries of the world for its cruelty and the difficulty of passing it, but in Syria, in the era of Assad regime, its reputation was even more cruel and ugly, so that everyone was talking about the death rate among the trainees through these courses and how it was officially permitted by the Assad regime, furthermore, the trainees were usually handled so brutally that those who have graduated from these courses maybe lose a part of their humanity, and this is exactly what the Assad regime always wanted and preferred, they want intelligence men to be killers and torture machines against people, moreover, to be persons with no mercy, no morals, and no emotions as well, then they do not care about kinships, friendships or any other human relations.

After completing all the required tests, in January 1994, the initiation date for our academic training beginning has been set; despite my natural tension in this situation, I was pleasant and self-confident because of what I've achieved so far which I considered as success. Previously, and since I was preparing to establish a secret organization against the regime, I had committed myself to strenuous exercises in the sport of body building in one of the clubs in my city Homs, it was Al Karama Sports Club, I always exercised this sport at home and everywhere all the time, I felt that I have a difficult future and responsibilities will not be easy to overcome, therefore,

I had to be committed by with a strict physical training in order to prepare myself to face these obstacles. It appeared later, that this idea was a blessing from Allah, Praise and thanks to him always.

In this period, when I completed my preparations to join the intelligence academic training, an important and historic incident took place in Syria which enhanced the belief in the existence of divine justice for the most of oppressed Syrians; the eldest son of Hafez al-Assad, Basel, was killed when he crashed in an accident on Damascus Airport road, according to the official version of the Assad regime at that time, this young man was the expected successor to his father Hafez, who was being prepared and trained publicly in full view of the Syrians and the world to inherit the empire of blood, hatred and sectarianism established by his father in Syria, and to continue in ruling the Syrian people coercively and unfairly, and without any consideration for the opinion, decision, and desires of this people.

The preparation of Basel for that role was running intensively and hastily in the last period before his death, because his father, the criminal Hafez, had a blood cancer for years, and all medical efforts that had been carried out by the Soviet Union, the first and the essential supporter for this criminal system, did not succeed in curing him, therefore, the death of his heir Basel was a great and unexpected shock to Hafez al-Assad and his sect and supporters as well. Although it is unacceptable for us as Syrian Sunni Muslim people to gloat over the death of any person, the Syrian people in general and particularly the oppressed people of Hama, who have been experiencing daily and over the previous years the pain of what the Assad regime did of killing, cutting and humiliating hundreds of thousands of their children and raped many of their daughters in front of them, they found themselves unable to stop their sense of happiness and gloating because of the realization of the divine justice when Hafez al-Assad tasted the same pain that he made the people to taste through the death of his most beloved, closest and most important son. People considered that what happened to his son, in addition to the severe deadly cancer he had along with the pain, the torment and the despair, all these maybe were a part of retributions from Allah against Hafez because of what he did.

Because of this significant event and due to the preoccupation of all the regime officers and officials with the consequences of this incident, the launch date of our training program at the Military Intelligence Academy, was postponed from January to the beginning of February 1994.

At this point, Allah has facilitated to me again a new thing, coupled with the providence that accompanied me throughout the implementation period of my plan, that is that one of the relatives of my mother, who had been staying with her family in Damascus for a long time, has good relations with the wife and the family of a senior officer from the Nusayri sect, who is not only a famous officer in an important position in the Military Intelligence administration, but also he was one of its founders in Syria, he is the Brigadier General Hani Al Abed, he was from those who participated in a large number of massacres against citizens in the capital Damascus and its countryside during the events of the Muslim Brotherhood Organization, he helped the Assad regime while disposing the members of this party in addition to all opponents of this regime by accusing everyone of belonging to the Muslim Brotherhood Organization, even if they don't know anything about that party, this accusation was sufficient to execute the accused immediately, without any trial according to terrible laws established and implemented by the regime of Assad the criminal, and continued to apply it throughout his period and that of his rogue son Bashar.

As results to the criminal efforts of Brigadier General Hani al-Abed in these fields, he was honored by being appointed commander of the Military Intelligence Academy, that is the main training and educational center for all military Intelligence officers, where I will be training.

I knew this information accidentally when I traveled at the first time to join the Intelligence academic training which has been postponed. I was disturbed because of this delay after the preparations that I did, thence, I visited our relative in Damascus, and when I explained to her where I was going, both of us were surprised by this coincidence that my training will be in a place directed by the neighbor and the family friend Brigadier General Hani.

Then they immediately called him by phone and asked him to help me as much as possible during the course; at that time, I realized the wisdom of Allah in this delay, which I was disturbed of it and thought it was evil {{But you may hate a thing although it is good for you, and may love a thing although it is evil for you}} Quran (2-216)

On the new launching date, I said goodbye to my family before I traveled to join the training program, in that time I didn't know if or when I will come back or if I'm even going to get exposed after I reached this level! Especially that I have to spend my daily life, for the first time in my life, among the enemies of mine and of my people, who hate me, and I hate them, who differ from me and I differ from them in everything!

After I had arrived to Damascus, I went to the central branch of the Intelligence Administration, where I found a large crowd of young people in the branch square, forthwith, I noticed the severity and cruelty of dealing with all of us from the first moment, whereas the shouting and rude handling used with all young people who will be sent to the academic and military training. They gathered us and forced us to sit on the dirty ground, then they threw bags that contain two suits of military clothing for each of us, thereupon, they crammed us in the boxes of military Russian-made trucks, thereafter, we were transported through the crowded streets of the capital until we arrived to a rugged mountainous area in Damascus countryside in a remote and not populated area, its name is Maysaloon, located very close to the Syrian-Lebanese border, It is known as one of the coldest areas in Syria, there and inside a small valley that almost disappears between the icy mountain peaks, they brought us into the Military Intelligence Academy which is the only one of its kind in Syria, meanwhile we crossed the walls and gates in the trucks that were taking us to our sector, I gazed at the different squares, I saw the first scenes of military life, there were young people running in regular rows on every road, in some corners there were some young trainees who had been stripped naked despite the harsh cold, others had their whole hair shaved while sitting on the muddy ground, at other corners, others were being punished by making them roll over the muddy and frozen ground or by putting them in dirty and cold water, when we arrived to our sector, shouting and insults began to fill the place around us then we discovered that it was directed to us from people who will be our trainers during the year that we will be here, and the disbelief and hatred words / cursing God and religions, which were very widespread among members of the Nusayri sect and an essential part of their speaking habits with or without any reasons, and all Syrians know that/, were heard from all the mouths around me and all persons either trainers or trainees, this was my first and most severe torment I always suffered from psychologically every day and every night for eighteen years later. It is not accepted by someone like me who grew up in a conservative society that respects all religions and sanctifies Allah Almighty and worship him and fear his anger all the time, to hear and coexist with the words of insult and cursing all the holy things, without any objection or reaction of any kind!

Then, newcomers like me were assembled, and divided into completely separated courses and sectors according to the scientific certificate of each of us, who have high school certification, they are the least number of applicants and I am one of them, we were separated from others and put in separate sleeping buildings, and they called us "Courses of cultured ", and the others who have elementary or preparatory certificates were also separated in other different sectors of the intelligence academy.

Since my first days in this course, I became sure that its bad reputation was not being exaggerated or being futilely circulated among people without reason. It was clear that it was designed to push the human body to the maximum of its endurance, and accustomed it to the harshest, ugliest and dirtiest conditions. So in the first days and weeks, when we started getting to know each other as new trainees, I noticed that the members of the Nusayri sect, despite that they seem to be unified against the other people, but they actually suffer from social and regional discrimination among themselves, so that the members of the Nusayri sect who live in the Syrian coast, because Assad and all his family and relatives belong to these areas, they are richer, more powerful, and closer to decision-makers, they were always flaunting and mocking the members of the Nusayri sect who are living in the Syrian interior regions, and most of them reside in the Homs and Hama villages and call them /Jiftlik/, which is an ancient ottoman word that means dry or hard land.

Sensitive centers and positions were often given to the Nusayris from the coast, whereas others are less standing than them and they are considered as followers moreover, I used this fact later to manipulate them, to feed this enmity and hatred among them, according to the rule that is (divide and conquer), which I have learned from them and from other repressive and colonial regimes that dominate the people after sowing discord among them. When the new trainees learned about my belonging to the residents of Homs city, they had the usual surprise, they assumed, because of their stupidity, that it is impossible for me to be from the Sunni sect and of course I have Nusayris origins. As I found them being reassured for this supposition, I did not deny it, and let them think like this, and I assumed that, in my early days among them and until I succeed in penetrating them, this might be better.

Despite that, and because of being the only one among them, as trainees, trainers and officers, who is from the city and not from the Countryside and rural areas, the matter that made them try to taunt me in the first weeks, and challenge me all, as they thought that my physical strength and my ability to endure difficulties will be weak, because the life in cities is so luxurious and easy that makes our bodies weak, flabby, and not strong and solid as the bodies of Countryside people who are used to work harder.

This challenge was a big motivation for me; hence my enthusiasm was increased. However, they did not know that I entered this place after I trained myself physically and psychologically for years, and that I have sufficient human and honorable reasons, and I carry an issue to remove the injustice from the people and Syrian society as well, that makes me ready more than them to endure everything and anything, as much as Allah Almighty will help me with it.

In fact, the training program at the Intelligence Academy had two main parts, all other details fall under them, they are:

1. Military and sports physical training, which was very cruel, and sometimes terrible.
2. Theoretical lessons and lectures, which are divided into two parts: the first; security intelligence topics, like: investigating, inspection, detention, protecting important persons, anti-drug, anti-spyware, rumors war, disguise, and opening locks ... etc.

The second; is the military and war lessons, like: the weapons with all kinds, the tactic, topography, military health, the reconnaissance, explosive materials, and the military law, ... etc.

Our military training was different from all other military armed forces in Syria, because it will be one of our tasks later to monitor all military units of all kinds in Syria, so we had to know information about all different military specialties and not study one military specialty, like other officers. But we had to be aware of and take a full and enough overview of all different kinds of the military specialties.

In fact, I did not have any problem with all of these types of training, thanks to Allah, although the other trainees repeatedly collapsed during training and most of them were crying sometimes, but I always was reminding myself that I am not like them, I didn't come here to loot and persecute the people, otherwise, my biggest problem was the extreme filth that surrounds me in all the details of life here, so I felt disgust of everything and everyone there. Actually, this was the major obstacle which is hard to be overcome in regard to me. However, a part of this filth was intentional by the Intelligence Academy Administration as a part of training to enhance the ability to overcome all kinds of difficulties; the other part of this filth came from the religious beliefs of the Nusayri sect, which is different from our beliefs, in reality, they do not believe that waste that comes out of human bodies as impure that need to be cleaned, for this reason the available bathrooms and toilets were submerged in human dirt which thickness reached more than five centimetres sometimes, moreover, the water we used was little and often frozen, so I often had to bathe by it, in sub-zero temperatures by more than 10 degrees during all winter, after training or using this water we all felt numb in our hands that is almost like a temporary paralysis; owing to this, we can't move it, we were even asking each other to close the military suit buttons of for each other while changing clothes quickly to go for the next training.

And even the restaurant where we eat all our meals, the tables there were being cleaned with the same mops that have been used for toilets and bathrooms, the dishes where the food was poured were disgusting, nonetheless, it smells bad. I used to see the wild animals coming from mountain at night to lick our dishes, then they used it to feed us without sterilization or cleaning. As a result of this extreme filth, which I never used to experience before, I was affected by an inflammation and severe chronic bleeding in the intestines, it stayed with me for a long time even after the training period.

The daily training program usually started before sunrise, where one of the trainers enters to the dormitories where we sleep, that are full of smells of filth from the sweated bodies and rotten socks of trainees as most of them didn't care about bathing in this terrible cold, thus, to avoid these smells, and to keep my bed clean and prevent the trainees from approaching and sitting on it, I chose an upper bed, of metal double-decker military beds, although the others preferred the lower bed for ease of use, moreover, I always opened one of the high windows above my bed during the night to relieve stinking smells despite the cold, rain and snow that might enter from this window to my cover and bed and make them wet, furthermore, this was always causing almost daily quarrels between me and the others who slept in the nearby beds, in the end, I had to secretly break the window so that no one would ask me to close it. The voice of the trainers was loudly and full of insults, cursing and disbelief expressions when they woke us up at this early time, moreover, they used, while waking us up, their hands, legs and ice water, and sometimes tough hoses or cables, to hit the sleepers, sometimes they may overturn the beds and the sleepers up to down, after waking up, we must keep running for the rest of the day until late at night, most days. As the first sports lesson was before breakfast, which is running semi-naked about three kilometers, wearing just sports shorts; actually, this was happening in a mountainous climate where the temperature is subzero throughout the winter. At these moments, we often saw steam emit from ice and snow when it touched us because of the heat of our bodies that just came out of the warmth of the bed.

We were running to the restaurant for breakfast, and even during the meal, it was from the common and lovely punishments from the officers to make us all eat our food while we were jogging in place next to dirty dining tables, there were no chairs to sit on it around these tables, so that we stayed a whole year eating our food in a squatting position around them. In fact, eating food in like these conditions in addition to the dirtiness of the food itself, was usually causing many trainees to vomit during the sport lesson that immediately follows the meal, without giving the trainee a short break to digest the food, so, as a result of that bad food situation, I remember that I stayed for months eating bread with some sweetness that I hold it and brought it with me by smuggling into the intelligence academy.

Then, we would run back to replace the sport suits with military uniforms and after that, go out to line up to go to the morning meeting and chanting slogans that glorify Assad, his party, and his regime. This meeting usually lasts about an hour, all the trainees of the training levels and sections, officers, staff, workers and recruits must attend this meeting, the penalties and usual dirty words were also attending.

When the meeting is over, the second sporting lesson begins which is harsher and longer than the first, and is not without of verbal and physical abuses as well; then the program of intelligence and military sciences classes and lectures begins, some of which are in the halls and others are in squares, mountains, and outdoors depending on the nature and requirements of those lessons. Then the lunch time, then the same program is repeated from sports and classes until the night and the end of dinner. Then it was supposed to be a break and to be able to do the personal needs of trainees, but the night was a fun time for officers and trainers to punish us, like: put us semi-naked in frozen dirty water, make us run for hours, and let us roll over the dirt and rubbish, or over the serrated gravel without shoes which leave painful wounds on the feet and bodies, the officers and trainers who do this are often very drunk.

During the first two months of the training period, I had very severe pain in my hands and rupture in the skin with a very dark color. During this period my family did not know anything about me, so my mother asked our former neighbor, Om Iyad, the officer's wife, to ask her husband to help her get permission to visit me at the intelligence Academy. Because Abu Iyad became an old officer with a high rank, it was not difficult for him to get this permission, so, one day, I was called during training time, I was surprised by my mother and the family of Abu Iyad waiting me all in the section dedicated for visits. My mother's grief and fear were great when she saw the sight of my hands that I mentioned, and she thought that I might have changed my mind, or I might realize that my coming here was a haste of a young son, they told me that I still have a chance to undo everything, because the leadership gives a choice for every volunteer like me to retreat during the first months of the training period only, this is called /abstention from the training /, so, my mother insisted on me to return with her, and this was also the opinion of the family of Abu Iyad, but I laughed from this idea to make my mother rest, I assured to her that I was fine, and I let them go back alone, and I stayed in my place.

After a while, when the intelligence academy doctor examined me, who was not accepting to examine any trainee unless his condition is very severe, he found that my hands have an illness called /frostbite/, which affects those who are exposed for very low temperatures for long periods of time, like mountain climbers, so that the symptoms of this infection are very similar to those of severe burns, Allah healed me after a period thanks to Him - the Almighty.

After a period from the course initiation, because of my superiority among others in sports and military training as a result of the preparations I had made in previous years, I was appointed as a general coordinator for all training sectors in the academy, this was an advantage such as military rank given to outstanding trainees or those close to one of the leaders, and become a supervisor at other trainees and assistant to trainers for organizing and controlling things. Throughout the next period of the training, I became responsible for training members of other sectors, who are inferior to us in rank and in their scientific certificate, in sports lessons and physical fitness. Of course, this matter and other causes made the hatred and envy against me increasing among the rest of my fellow trainees and some trainers as well, so they consequently made numerous attempts to harm me in various ways even by establishing a conglomerate against me, moreover, they were repeatedly doing that until the end of the training period, but I had prepared myself from the moment I entered this place for this possibility, so I worked at inflaming the differences and regional sensitivities that are already present among them, and Allah helped me in transforming our sector and our dormitory into completely scattered groups, for example: a group for the people from Safita and Drakeish area, a group for the people from Jabla area, a group for the people from Banias and Tartus, and my group was the largest and most powerful of all, It is a group for the people from the central region of Syria: Homs and Hama and their countryside, of course all of them were from the Nusayri sect, and in all volunteer sectors at the Military Intelligence Academy at that time, whose number was about 1200 people, there was only I and another young man from the Sunni majority, the other young man was from Areha area in the countryside of Idlib city, he is a simple and good-hearted young man his extreme poverty prompted him to volunteer with us, I remained, throughout the training period, trying to protect him from the harm of others.

And when we had regular exams at the end of every three months of the training in all intelligence and military sciences materials, I always, thank to Allah, got top marks and ranked first of the class.

Three months before the end of the training period something important happened that I should mention, after we have finished the penultimate exams, after which we get a period of vacation normally, its duration is one week we usually spend as a rest in our family homes, and because of the bad marks that a lot of our sector trainees got, the leader of our training, who was one of the most malicious characters I saw in this place, issued an order to deny us all from the vacation, even though we haven't been given any vacation for a long time, and we were eagerly awaiting that, furthermore, he did not exclude, from his sentence, those who got good grades in the exam like me, and not only that but he also ordered of spending the vacation time in penalties managed by our trainers. Then I had an idea that I implemented immediately, namely: Why do not I perform the first test of my disruptive abilities on enemies and control of their minds here, especially, after I have made prestige to myself and well-heard opinions among them all!?

And really, following the decision of our training leader and during lunch, I started inciting everyone who were already angered by his unjust decision, I said to them: how do you accept this and why are you silent about it!?

How do you accept injustice after all the fatigue and effort you have made!?

They said: what can we do!?

I said: rebel and reject the error.

They said: How do?

I answered them: If any of us violate the orders, it will be easy to punish him, but if we all agree and pledged to fulfill, we can do whatever we want.

They said: good, what exactly shall we do!?

I told them: We all will run away at the first break, from over the walls of the academy which we are guarding part of it, and we can get out of this part, then we will go through the forests and mountains around us, where no car can get in and catch us up, until we arrive to any village then we take a bus back to the capital, from there each of us travels to his city, therefor, in order that none of us betrays his colleagues or come back before them, and be punished by the trainers, we must swear by everything we believe in and our honor to come back on a specific day and hour, thus, the guilt is divided among all members of the course, So doing, none will be punished because it is not possible to punish a whole sector, this matter has never happened before /that's what I convinced them with, of course/, and we agree that who is betraying our covenant will be an enemy of us all, also, he will be a target for sarcasm from everyone because he is a traitor and has no enough manhood characters.

Indeed, everyone responded to my incitement, and we defined a place and a time to meet after a week, the duration of the vacation we have decided for ourselves, and we pledged in spite of our knowledge that who will run away with us can't break his covenant because if he returns before others, the anger of the training leader and trainers and perhaps the anger of the academy leadership will be imposed on him alone, and then our anger as colleagues. Indeed, the implementation was quick and accurate, from all course members, except one trainee named Yahya, he feared and retreated at the last moments before we jumped over the walls, and he returned, this accursed person eliminated me almost, but Allah saved me, so what are the details of that !?

In fact, for us, the plan went very well, we have been running fast in the forests for a while so that no one can catch us up, finally, we reached a highway and boarded the first bus and crammed ourselves all in it. When we arrived in Damascus, each of us continued to travel to his city. For me I was delighted with victory; I accomplished my first mission in the enemy house. I manipulated them and their minds and I led their rebellion against one another, and against their laws, moreover, I deceived them as they deceived my people many times, I planted the first discord among them, the matter that didn't just happen anywhere, but among their clever and trained men who they rely on them, thus I gained an extra confidence by myself, in addition to a pleasant vacation with my family.

But, later we knew that what we did /or what I instigated and did/, according to what the trainers told us later, is the first historical event of its kind in the Syrian intelligence service since its establishment, and that our experience will remain for many years to be told to all new trainees and trainers about a whole sector that escaped from the academy for one week. The trainers told us that they were completely stunned when they realized that we run away, so that they didn't know what to do, but they investigated with Yahya immediately, who told them what we agreed on verbatim. Then the trainers notified the duty officer, who, in turn, mobilized all the cars of the intelligence academy to track us on all the public roads that surround the place, they had no idea that I had planned and chose the forest path to escape. The trainers also told us that in the day after our escape during the morning meeting, in which each sector leader usually offers a result of the inspecting of his trainees and the number of absences among them and the reasons to the academy leader (who was a Brigadier general), and instead of the usual shout of our course leader that there is no absence and it is ready, this time he was forced to shout that all members of the high school graduates sector are illegally absent. And when he said this, as I mentioned earlier, he is an arrogant officer and everyone hates him, at first everyone was stunned and the academy leader asked him to repeat what he said, and when he repeated that his whole course was absent, then all the officers laughed at him and ridiculed him, even the academy leader, and what we have done has become a stigma in his history and work record.

   Later, we knew that the only traitor of our plan, Yahya, told them that I was the instigator and the leader of this rebellion. Again, as usual, the hand of God's care intervened to protect me, because what we did humiliated and insulted the leader of our sector in front of everyone, he made a proposal to the academy leader to make me face penalty in Palmyra Military Prison (Tadmur) which is classified as one of the dirtiest and most awful and deadly prisons in the world, but the commander of the intelligence academy, Brigadier General Hani, who as I mentioned has a good relationship with the family of one of my relatives, rejected this suggestion completely, he told our sector leader that he was allowed to do whatever he wanted when we return, but only within the academy, then Brigadier General Hani called my relative's house with a laugh and he told them that he saved me from the evils and hatred of my commander who submit a complaint against me that I am the leader and instigator of this rebellion, the charge that could have possibly destroyed my future.

When we returned on the agreed date, the leader of our sector was waiting for us and prepared a program of punishments and torture for a month, he did not leave any punishment come to mind unless he tries it with us, he prevented us from wearing clothes for a whole month, every day, he rolled us over the trash, human waste, and thistle bushes, of course, he always intended to increase these punishments to me. Fortunately, the summer season has begun and the weather is getting warmer, but, as a result of the implementation of sanctions on us under the hot sun and for long hours, I and a group of young men had swollen skin under the hair, and suppuration in this region. When the academy doctor examined us, he told us it was a mild case of a very serious disease called meningitis, and without the mercy of Allah and that we took a vaccines against this disease before, the situation would have been dangerous and deadly, the doctor ordered us to wear military hats during the sanctions against us, and asked us to wet them continuously.

Thanks to Allah, after few days, the skin that was swollen in our heads began to peel and fall, this was a sign of healing.

As a result of all the exercises, diseases, and the harsh conditions that I described during this training period, I felt that I gained strength, immunity, and resistance so that the sanctions never affect me no matter how strong it was, I was laughing during punishment time so that our vicious sector leader noted this. I remember that during the execution of one of the sanctions against us, we were doing a hard exercise and putting our hands into serrated gravel, all trainees were screaming of pain and begging the leader of the training to stop this punishment, I was easily doing the exercise, and whenever I notice that the training leader is watching me I became, I meant to challenge this officer, to show him my endurance, and that his sanctions do not affect me, by doing the exercise very quickly and just by my fingers, not by my hands, then, I noticed the extreme anger looked on his face, thereupon, he stopped the sanction, and shouted, addressing the rest of the trainees -they are all of his Nusayri sect members-, you dogs, you thugs, you bastards your training period is nearly completed and no one gets benefit from it, only this young man has become stronger, and mentioned my name and my nickname, but what I and everyone understood, and he could not say, that he meant this Sunni, son of the city, who we thought him to be weak, he overcomes you all, you are the rural strong people and the people of my sect. Then I was very pleased and proud, because it is a testimony from the mouths of the leaders and trainers of our enemies themselves, that I triumphed over them thanks to Allah.

During this training period, I gained a weight about 20 kilograms of muscle mass, my physical appearance has changed completely, and of course my whole life changed after that. At the end of February 1995, we were graduated from the training period. Our leader instead of saying goodbye to us as usually supposed, he gave us a lecture that we were the most riotous trainees group of his life, and that he hates us, and predicts a bad future for us, and of course we, especially me, were hardly resisting laughter because we knew that he speaks to us like this due to his anger from us and what we caused to him of humiliation and embarrassment among the other officers, he even refused to send buses with us to transport us to Damascus as usual and we were forced to walk long distances to find transportation, it was a revenge on us.

I was informed that I got the first place on all my peers in all intelligence and military sciences examinations - thanks to Allah - and this was recorded in my file that will accompany me at the State. At the end of the course, when we were asked to hand over all the notebooks we were using in study, and write all the security and intelligence lessons in it, I hid my books, notebooks and pamphlets after I deluded them that I delivered it like the others, because I thought I could benefit from it to train members of our secret organization about the intelligence missions, these notebooks and pamphlets remained hidden in my home until 2012, when my house was bombed and destroyed by the regime of criminal Bashar al-Assad during the blessed Syrian Revolution that year, and burnt with the rest of the house and other papers, (and because we always as Muslims accept our destiny, I just said thanks to Allah anyway and in all circumstances).

The intelligence training is finally over, I did it, I am the ordinary young man who comes from an ordinary family of the Sunni majority, I officially became a trained and qualified employee in the Syrian Military Intelligence Service, the forces that had contributed in injustice, persecution, and subjugating millions of my countrymen, of my religion, and my society. I succeeded in penetrating the enemies of the Syrian people, these wicked fools trained me using their potential, efforts, and money on things and experiences that will be an extra weapon with me that I will use in my secrecy wars against them, and I have in fact succeeded in this for seventeen years with the help of Allah.

The shocking surprise and the hard-fateful decision!

During the training-end leave, while I was waiting for the assortment result, which will determine in any intelligence branch will each trainee work, as there were many branches that are led by the military intelligence administration, distributing in Damascus and all Syrian cities and regions; in that time, I began my attempts to renew the meetings with my friend Ahmad and my group's members who were our partners in our secret organization; knowing that the meetings between me and all others, including Ahmad, during the year that I spent in the intelligence academy, minimized in numbers, and were nearly nonexistent with the other members of the group due to various reasons; for example, because the vacations were very rare in the training time, moreover, we knew that we must be very cautious since I was very likely to be under a secret monitoring by the regime agents and spies after being working with them. However, when I had met Ahmad, I started to notice that his behavior with me changed, I could not recognize these changes exactly in the beginning; not only Ahmad but all other friends as well. Ahmad no longer liked to meet me separately, and was always avoiding talking about our organization by changing the direction of the discussion or by making this idea look absurd by turning it into joking, furthermore, I noticed that new guys joined our group; they were ordinary young persons who were different from us; according to their talking I knew that this was happening all my absence time while I was at the academy.

Our meetings, our discussions, and our concerns became far away from public issues, politics, and religious affairs! So that the conversations became about playing cards, football matches, girls, and all what usually concern the guys in this age. Furthermore, the more I attempted again and again to return the seriousness to our discussions and redirect them to their right direction, like before, the more my astonishment became bigger due to the insistence of Ahmad and the others and their avoidance of this matter. Unfortunately, after months of repeating the attempts, the new shocking fact became clear enough for me, as I knew that all the group, including Ahmad, either with or without agreement, cancelled everything that we agreed on and about previously; moreover, they were avoiding the topic at all or even mentioning the reasons. I felt that they are other persons who are completely different from those I know and trusted them before, those who I sacrificed my life, my future, my family, my reputation, and my comfort for what we agreed on and about and for what we built together. I analyzed the possible reasons that pushed them to retreat, is it the fear which was planted long ago inside their parents' and their own hearts and in everyone from our people from the violence and criminality of the intelligence services? Did that make them afraid of me because I became a member of that service? Did they think that I might, after all what I did for our plan, betray them? Or they expected me to get discovered and fall in the hands of our enemies, in which case they all may be get exposed and even face mortal danger?

Or perhaps the fear wasn't at all the reason behind their retreatment from our organization, maybe they were not serious from the beginning, as they were basically not eligible since they were too young and without capabilities to undertake such mission; moreover, their response maybe was a youth caprice and a desire for excitement within the borders of speeches and dreams which they were not ready to realize and implement due to their dangerous consequences; or they were driven behind the youths' tendencies and followed their lusts, pleasures and entertainment that fit their age like others; and left the matter of reform and resistance for the unknown like other millions of the humiliated people.

What I knew and was sure of was that some of them had some of these reasons while most of them had all these reasons together.

When I became sure of all what I previously explained, I felt as if a had a deep painful wound, moreover, I felt, for a period, like being lost and that I was betrayed what made me lose my own future as a price I had to pay for; in that time, there was no escape from having to stop for a while and review my choices and judge for myself, then it was necessary to take a decision and put a new plan.

What did I do to myself!

I've thrown myself into the den of my archenemies who fight all what I believe in. Of course, without any possibility or way to withdrawal, as all Syrians know that, regarding to the Assad regime, all who work in security and intelligence services will not be allowed to resign or leave the job at all, whatever they try, and they are not allowed to travel also; so that quitting the job was possible in two cases only, the first one is to have a permanent or severe disability that makes the person not useful for any job, while the second is the death.

What is the benefit from joining this service now after I became completely alone, of course, I no longer have any possibility to recruit or add any new persons to my organization in the future; the reason is: How will it happen! If my best trustful friends became afraid of me and they ran away and retreated! ; How will that be possible again now!, after I have military rank that could frighten any citizen in Syria and made me look like a human monster which is a traitor and there is no way to trust him, furthermore, all my words, in term of regime opposition, will be considered as a trap to discover the intentions of people against the regime; as almost all people, except few who know the truth and the real factors, believe that I become faithful to this regime and that I'm working for it.

Even if I continued my plan, i.e. working as a subversive spy and secret enemy against the regime from inside, could I, as one person with limited abilities and capabilities, effectively be useful for my case and harmful to my enemies as I wish and desire?! My plan was to support other persons in joining intelligence and state bodies, so the more our number increase the easier our mission will be. However, I asked myself, did I commit a crime and make a big mistake against myself by sacrificing for those who don't deserve?!

The more important than all these questions is what should I do now?!

I was pretty sure of myself, as I mentioned to you before, that my intention, when starting this work, was good and aims to obey Allah; according to my knowledge, everybody who is honest and has a good intention, he will not be disappointed at all. The easiest solution and the logical answer for my questions that everyone in my situation will be persuaded with is that the best thing I can do is to forget about all my previous thoughts and plans and start to track my personal interests, especially that now the life's doors with all its pleasures were open in front of me and for free by working in the intelligence services where the unlimited competencies, capabilities, and power were given to its officers. But doing so, that means I throw all my principles, values, moralities, and my religion; beside throwing the revenge of my people as well as the blood of martyrs, and follow the same devil road that the regime and his followers follow and are trying to pull Syria as whole to it.

When I reached this point of thinking, I took a fateful decision regarding my life, my method, and my upcoming plan, it was one way decision, thus, I decided to be and stay, as I planned previously, a spy, not for my previous organization which was failed by the other's fear, and not for any other party or specific side, but for nobody, yes I decided to work as a spy for nobody in particular, and for everybody from my society, my religion, and my people. If God Will, I'll gather the information and store it then I'll give it to those who need it from the oppressed people or the honest opponents of this regime, in case finding them. I'll fight my enemies inside their home, I'll subvert, and plant the seeds of affliction and segregation among them, I'll create rumors and distribute them in order to enhance the negative feelings and opinions that will hurt them, and I'll promote the negligence and carelessness of the duties among them. Indeed, God helped me to successfully continue doing these tasks and many others without being discovered for 16 years in the intelligence service, and for two further years in the Assad army as well, so Praise be to God, the mastermind of everything.

The years of working in the Military Intelligence Branch in Hama

After the end of the academic study and training, and after finishing my vacation, I went to the administrative branch of the intelligence service in Damascus, where I got the assortment report that will determine my new work place, which was the Military Intelligence Branch in Hama, the devastated and oppressed city that is located near to my city Homs, actually, Hama story generated my story, and its tragedy and devastation were pushing me forward. In that time, I did not feel that it was a strange coincidence, as it might seem to be, but I felt that it was a new arrangement, facilitation and conciliation from Allah Almighty.

When I was taking the bus to Hama, the city that I didn't know well before, I noticed the horror and confusion on the faces of the driver and the passengers just because I asked them where is the intelligence branch and where should I get off the bus. Upon arriving, I found a huge and very high fence almost hiding all buildings behind it, it surrounds a very vast land, and around that fence there was a hoop of cemented blocks and others fewer high fences. From outside view, the branch was not like any other intelligence branch that I've ever see elsewhere; it looks like an ancient castle that protects kingdoms and kings inside, but it is now protecting the criminals; despite the wholly destruction of Hama and killing, displacing, and arresting almost all its population by the Assad regime, they were still afraid of the consequences of what they did before, and from any possible revenge that might happen in any moment. After passing all these various gates and guardians, by showing my ID and my mission papers for everyone and at every gate, I submitted myself to the registry office that specialized in registering the new members; then, they told me that I must wait for days or maybe for weeks to meet the Chief of the branch who is the only one who has the authority to determine in any department or office I will work in

I started immediately asking all officers I met about the name and specifications of each department in the Branch, finally, I decided attempting to join to the IT department (computers); in fact, my choice was based on many rational reasons that make this place the best for me, as, there, I'll be able to get a huge amount of information, data, secrets, decisions, and mails among the leaders of the Assad regime and the Branch; because all what I mentioned is being sent or receipted via IT department, in addition to the second reason, which was very important to me, that if I work in this department I'll be automatically absolved from being compelled to act like the officers of other department who participate directly in oppressing and persecuting or torturing people. Indeed, by working in IT department, I'll avoid killing people like what is more likely happening in other departments like Judicial Investigation Section and Prison Section. Lastly, I preferred to work in this department because I knew that the chief of the department is the engineer officer lieutenant colonel Mohammed Deeb, who has a calm character and is less vicious than others. Actually, I began asking and looking for a way and mediation which could enable me to communicate with this officer and ask him to bring me to work in his department. By researching, I had known that one of my uncles (brother of my mother), who worked previously as a member of one of the medical military committees, helped Ltn colonel to get the approval on the demobilization request for his father, therefore, Ltn colonel Mohammed promised my uncle to help him one day. I was very happy when I knew this story, then, my uncle gave me a recommendation letter to Ltn colonel Mohammed asking him to help me and make me join me his department; thus, I met him and gave him the letter and told him my desire, but his answer was to wait the result of my interview with the Brigadier Chief of the Branch.

What happened taught me the first lesson about how the relationships and work stream are going on in the Syrian Intelligence Services, where I noticed, duo to what happed and many others events later, that the military ranks and the position's degrees were not more than formalities within the Syrian Intelligence Services at the Assad regime, moreover, they were not with actual value among the officers and individuals inside the Branch, while as the true actual value was determined by the degree of the support and the power of the mediation that every person within the branch already has. Among the Nussayris themselves, this equation of power was affected by how much the person is close or far from Assad family members or from the families of other senior officials and decision makers in this regime. Furthermore, those who were working with or under the power of some close persons who have power and authorities, duo to above mentioned reasons, were enjoying much more power and influence, therefore, many individuals, non-commissioned officers, or even civil employees, whom I met during my work in the intelligence, had power, competencies, authorities, and influence that were not available for those who have higher ranks and positions. In Hama, and for a long time, there were many civil employees who had not any military or intelligence rank, and were not even educationally qualified, despite that all, they were assigned as leaders of intelligence groups responsible of securing and monitoring many large regions and villages; while as there were many ranked and qualified officers working in the branch who were annotated and assigned for simple and not valuable tasks.

After some days, Major General Ahmad Halloom, the Chief of the Branch, interviewed me and all new officers separately. My interview was quick and lasted only few minutes, the chief was such a huge man with a criminal appearance, the color of his face was strange as if he was not exposed to sunshine for a very long time. During the interview, he asked me some quick questions about my life, qualifications, and family, while he was scanning my face precisely by his eyes. However, after finishing the interview and getting out his office, I was informed that I was assigned to work in the Information department in the branch.

In fact, when they informed me the result, my feelings were divided between discomforts from failing to join the computer department, and satisfaction when I knew that the chief of information department is one of the very few officers who belong to the Sunni majority who still kept their positions after they proved their absolute faithfulness and blind obedience to the Assad regime, and they supported that evidence by blood shedding of the Syrian citizens in general and the Sunni Muslims particularly. This officer was the most famous one and the closest to the Assad regime, he is the Colonel Mohammad Alsha'ar, who has, as I knew, a big influence and a wide reputation among all groups of normal

Syrian citizens and military workers because of his "achievements" and services during the events of Muslim Brotherhood in Hama 1982, while he was working in the Intelligence Branch in Homs, through participating in arresting and torturing thousands of people from well-known families there; usually, those people were religious men, educated persons, or students in Homs city after charging them with belonging or commiserating with the Muslim Brotherhood; and many of them were executed secretly by the regime.

After that period, Colonel Mohamad, when he had lower rank, participated in the oppression and persecution against the Lebanese people after he was transferred to the Syrian Military Intelligence Branch during the occupation period of the Lebanese Republic by the Assad regime. Whereas, he and other intelligence officers were arresting many Lebanese citizens in attempting to kneeling and subjugating the Lebanese people; they also participated in looting the money and properties of that nation. Due to these valuable criminal services to the Assad regime, Colonel Mohamad's influence increased, and he had become more powerful within the regime. But I had thought that he will be the best for me, as we were from the same religious group, in spite of this bad reputation; or else I'll be forced to work in another department where the chief is Nussayri, and definitely he would then direct his sectarian hatred toward me.

After I was assigned to the information department, and already joined, some officials told me that I must wait for a few days to interview Colonel Mohamad, the Chief of the department. Indeed, after a short time, he made an interview with me, which was like the previous ones nominally, but in term of content, it was entirely different from my point of view, as I was very curious to see one of the greatest traitors that have the highest positions and ranks from the people of my religion, what he looks like and how his personality is!.

In fact, I was totally surprised when I saw him because I imagined that I would see a man with a huge athletic body at least according to his reputation and also as it was well-known that the physically fit body was a precondition for being accepted in the army, he looked very arrogant and haughty; he was always smoking an expensive cigar. I felt that this man knew very well that he would never have such power and influence, even in his best dreams, without the corruption and perversion of the Assad regime which was advancing his men the more they increased their crimes, filthiness and inhumanity. Because of that, this Colonel and all those who were like him, were adherence to serve this regime as they knew that if the regime gets collapsed their right place would be among the scum of the society.

I surely felt during the interview that I was not the only one who was curious; but he was also the same, I noticed that from his gazes and questions; especially that he worked in Homs, my city, for many years, and he knows very well the status of my family as well as the characteristics of the people there, their boycotting of the Assad regime, and their hidden secret hatred against this regime. While I was standing in front of him, on the other side of the table, and despite of being from the same society, origin, and religious group, but I knew very well that I and him were completely contrary; as there is a vast difference between who spent his age betraying his people and serving a dictatorial regime and assisting it, and who sacrificed and risked their lives and everything in attempt to help and support their oppressed people.

After the interview, they inform me that I was appointed in the worker's office (economic office) in the information department, which was specialized in following and monitoring all factories, companies, institutions, and banks that belong to the civilian and governmental sector and the private sector as well. Whereas this office was monitoring and interfering in all the affairs of the governmental employees, from the general manager down to the office employee, during the working hours or even in his personal life with his family. Like all the security and intelligence branches in Syria, the powers granted to interfere in the affairs of the citizens had no borders and no limits.

I was so happy and content because I will work in the economic office, again, I felt it was a new reconciliation from God Almighty; especially when I realized that I could direct my work there against the thieves and defalcators, and being far away from participating in oppressing and persecuting the people just because they practice their freedom and religious actions, or they criticized an official, as it will usually happen if I work in other offices which are specialized in monitoring the religious, political, and military affairs.

The first period in the economic office was a training stage, I worked in this office within the branch for many weeks, I was learning, in this period, how the work is going on, what are the subjects of interests, and how we should deal with them. Actually, the first thing that attracted my attention is the considerable levels of corruption among the officers of this office and the branch as a whole. Obviously, in their conversation and behaviors, there was no appreciation to honor, morals, work fellowship, or even their belonging to the same sect; only those who presented foods and money, to their chiefs and to the higher ranked officers, get all what they want. Of course, the source of all these money, gifts, and foods, which is circulated among the officers and employees as a bribery, was from stealing and extorting the citizens in Hama, and from haggling those poor people on their life and life of their children. The administrative employees, who work always in the branch headquarter and they are not allowed to leave their place during the working hours, were the responsible officers for distributing the tasks and the work plans and submitting mails to the chiefs of departments. Because those employees were not allowed to work and communicate with citizens like other officers (city officers), they hated them and envied them, as the administrative employees thought that they were prohibited from a valuable treasure which is the pockets and money of the citizens in Hama. Consequently, they in turn extort and bargain the city officers over their sharing of the spoils stolen daily from the people in exchange for services, such as changing the distribution of tasks according to the interests of the briber and the bribed, and improving or distorting the image of the city's officers in front of the higher-ranking officers and in front of the head of the branch, or sometimes covering up the delay or failure of some officers or their mistakes in their work.

The greatest concern that everyone shows in their conversations and work after the money topic is the consumption of alcohol and prostitution even in the branch headquarters and during the working hours. Actually, the bottles and glasses of alcohol were everywhere and in every office and department, they drink strong alcohol all the day like water, furthermore, there were prostitutes and women who were dragged into sexual relations with officers under multiple pressures, such as extortion, threats, etc., they were brought in or summoned publicly and almost daily to everyone's offices. Therefore, all the conversations among the officers, employees, and workers of the branch were about these dirty behaviors, they were proud in doing and practicing these actions. It was from the mercy of God Almighty that I met a young man from my Sunni group, who joined the branch in the same period that I joined and in the same place, he was from the Damascus countryside; however, he was, at first, almost like the others in terms of the level of his corruption and moral decay, but since he belongs to a respected family and his parents were good persons and brought him up on the good moralities, he was always suffering from constant struggle between good and evil inside himself, later, this guy, Haytham, and throughout all the long days and years of my work in the Military Intelligence, became my only friend and my fellow in this place and this dirty infested atmosphere. Since the first years, he proved that he had become better and higher moral than those dirty people who work with us, so that I considered him like a brother, we were partners in almost everything, except my hidden and dangerous secret, I had never told him about that.

During this period also, they were, in the Intelligence Branch in Hama, updating and correcting the information of so-called (Fugitives' studies), which are dossiers and files containing full information and data about tens of thousands of Hama citizens who escaped and survived from death that was chasing them at the hands of Assad's executioners during and after Hama Massacre events; in that time, those people completed their surviving journey by crossing the borders into neighboring countries like Jordan and Iraq, in fact, most of them except a few number never had any relation with the Muslim Brotherhood Party, nor with the Hama Massacre events except the harm and injustice that was done to them in that period. However, the criminals of Assad regime did not like to let anyone to escape from their evilness, so that he become a witness about what they did in the city; for this reason, they started to prepare these files called the (Fugitives' studies), they were about six thousand dossiers, in which the main charge was the affiliation with the Muslim Brotherhood Party; whereas the penalty of this accusation, as was prescribed in the unjust law laid down by the Assad regime, was the immediate execution without investigation or trial.

In these studies, they wrote down full information about the accused persons, that they will fabricate the accusations for, in addition to mentioning the names of all their family members and relatives up to the fifth degree with extra information about those as well. Many of those relatives were still living in Hama, consequently, those poor miserable people were being periodically recalled to the branch for more than 25 years just because they were mentioned in these studies. There, they were humiliated, intimidated and blackmailed under the pretext of interrogating them and asking them about the latest news of their fugitive relatives; this is something that no one has heard or known of injustice like it in any country or other system throughout the history, by holding someone accountable for an accusation that a distant relative was accused of, and that he remains subject to persecution dozens of years for this.

Furthermore, all the population of Hama were treated as second-class citizens during the period of the criminal Hafez Al-Assad authority; they were not allowed to be employed in the military and civil employments, it was also absolutely impossible in the intelligence functions; they were also vulnerable to persecution, bad treatment, and contempt from the regime's followers everywhere in the state or government; moreover, only being a citizen from Hama was similar to having a charge or a crime that make you feel afraid and shy from people in the Assad era. Not only that, but when I was asked to participate in updating these studies, as they were not updated for more than 12 years, what I read in these studies, from injustice and the sorrowful details about the Hama tragedy and the massacres that were committed by the regime's executioners, were unbelievable. What had been done by the Assad regime and its men, along with those who were brought from Nussayri villages, was not only unbelievable but also it was such devil actions that could not be imagined by the normal humankind; it was furthermore more cruel than the animals' and monsters' behaviors as well. This coincidence that made me aware of this dangerous information, from the beginning of my work in this branch, as well as my knowledge of the amount of cruel injustice and racial cleansing which our people in Hama suffered from, had a great impact on myself and a new and strong motivation for me to follow up on my plan and my conviction increased about its importance to the people if God gave me the strength to continue to implement it.

My work on these files and studies was the first task I successfully carried out against this regime, thanks to Allah, that instead of checking and correcting the data included in these studies by investigating the mentioned people, as I was supposed to do, and as the others officers did; I forged, changed, and altered a lot of information and data, which, due to the large number of studies, was difficult to be detected, where I changed ages for many names, and I changed the degrees that others hold, and I exchanged residence addresses outside Syria and in the neighboring countries that I mentioned before, the total number of what I succeeded in forging at the time was about four hundred files. Although an officer checked it after I finished, my work was being approved and saved in the branch information as it is.

Those who have no experience may think that exchanging this simple information is of little value, but in reality it might be a reason to save human lives, because if any person mentioned in these studies is caught or arrested, the difference between his information and that in the branch, may prevent his execution, and if his luck is good, he will be released because of the information mismatch, and I have done this many times over the following years, every time the studies of those fleeing were updated, as usual many hundreds of them are being delivered to me, in addition, I was pretending that I help the Nusayri officers in updating their studies, then I manipulated these studies as I like, and they were very pleased and thanked me for what they thought was help from me, especially that a large number of the officers of this branch and of the Intelligence administration in general were only holding a false primary certificate that the regime was giving it to them in their regions, as they themselves told me, in order to be able to obtain the minimum requirements to get an employment in the Syrian security and intelligence services, so, they could barely write and poorly read, however, they did not need knowledge or competences in their work in this system, all what they need is the ability to do injustice, repression, theft and extortion. So they were very pleased when I help them with a lot of writing works, also they always asked me to do so, and this gave me, by the grace of Allah, greater ability to see and manipulate the content of intelligence topics and reports and change it for the benefit of citizens, and to mitigate the harm at them as much as my possibilities allowed, and it made me more in control of these officers because they needed me, and their fear of my knowledge about their mistakes because of what I mentioned.

After a period of training at the branch headquarter, the Colonel, the chief of the department sorted and determined my work as a field investigator in Hama /City officer / within the economic field, the specialty of the economic office where I work, and commissioned a Nusayri officer, named Suhail Khalil, to train me to work in Hama by accompanying me every day on his patrols to the governmental departments, that he was charged with monitoring and controlling, as each city officer was being handed a sector of the governmental departments, that he will be responsible in front of the leadership of the branch to inform them about all what is happening in these departments, by providing intelligence reports, that the officer writes in the end of every day, and presents it to the commanding officers in the branch, this sector usually consists of a geographically contiguous group of factories, institutions, professional and scientific unions, popular organizations, administrative directorates, and all the places where government sector employees work, whereas each city officer moves in his sector daily from one factory to another, and from one directorate to another, according to what the working time permits, and the part that he could not visit due to insufficient time, he calls and knows what he wants by phone.

The story of the first officer who trained me, Suhail Khalil, was one of the strangest stories I saw in the Hama Intelligence branch, even he was telling it to everyone, and always amazed of it, and he mocked himself in front of everyone, this officer, although he was working in the branch of Hama for a long time, what made him an experienced officer may be in the eyes of the leaders, he did not get any school certificate in his lifetime, not even a primary school certificate, and he had barely learned to read and write, despite this, he was in charge of and responsible for the Medicine Union, the National Hospital, the Nursing School in Hama, the Engineers Union, and the Lawyers Syndicate and the Judicial Palace / this place where all courts, judges and the Public Prosecution Office existed in Syria, is named like that/, in other words, he was in charge of monitoring, following up, checking, investigating, and keeping up with daily discussions with the persons of the highest academic degrees in Syria. When I met him, this responsibility has been going for almost twelve years, after that, he continued to do this work for about fifteen years, and he was making fun of this matter, and always said to other officers in the branch mocking this matter: Did the state not found someone less knowledgeable and cultural than me to assign him to deal with holders of the highest academic and university degrees in Hama!!?

I have accompanied Suhail in his patrols for several months in order to learn how to work in Hama, and the way of the intelligence service dealing with civil government departments and companies.

The first thing that surprised me when I started the field work in Hama, and after I patroled among the citizens and the civil employees with Suhail during his intelligence work, is the unlimited powers and the absolute authority of intelligence personnel over the citizens of all groups and affiliations. Although I had previously known, heard and seen a lot during my life, as a Syrian youth or as a school student and a Syrian citizen, about the strength of the powers of the intelligence services and their control over people, but when I became one of them, I discovered that almost everything was permitted to intelligence personnel in the era of Hafez al-Assad, in addition to having almost complete immunity from statutory and judicial accountability for any offense they commit. This was the general situation at the time all over Syria, however, the very special conditions of the city of Hama and the horrors that the regime did to it and what it continued to do, (just as I explained to you several parts of that strange situation earlier), made any intelligence officer in Hama possessing influence and powers more than that of his counterparts in other cities, the Hama people were treated by the regime as second-class citizens, traitors, betrayers, and as enemies of the criminal Assad regime, therefore, intelligence forces were required to continue humiliating and subjugating them, and the example that was common and always used by senior officers and leaders of intelligence and they always recommended it to the officers as a wisdom that must be adhered to and acted upon, They say:

"The people of the city of Hama are like a metal spring, as long as you are stepping on it and fastening it with your feet, you are safe. But if you ever think about lifting your feet from them, this spring will bounce and jump to hit your face and harm it".

On the other hand, it was permitted to the officers, as a satanic reward, to enjoy all what they can get from the poor people of Hama, in any dirty way these officers want, in short, the intelligence services in Syria in general and in Hama in particular, were armed looting gangs, that were protected and backed by the authority of the sectarian law, when Suhail and I were entering any union, directorate, or institution, everyone and even the managers stood in fear, terrified, and they often made us sit on their desk, we rarely heard the word "no" on any request we made from any citizen, we could just simply have shared them on their cars, their money, their homes, and everything they own, in addition to the bribes that were called gifts, also, invitations to luxurious banquets and regular or lewd night parties were provided to Suhail and other intelligence personnel almost always. And whoever dares to refuse the wishes of any intelligence officer, his life can be turned into hell, through the ability of this officer to fabricate deathly charges for all in simply, or by dismissing any employee from his work, or by setting pressure on him until he is forced to resign from his job and become without a source of livelihood.

Moreover, all landline telephones in Syria, which were available at that time, were always all-day 24 hours monitored by the military intelligence, and because of this, the Intelligence administration was exploiting people's personal secrets, and used slips of their tongue that they say on their landline telephone calls (which was the only way to communicate in Syria at that time) against them, to blackmail them and control them much more. Even people who were considered responsible in the state in front of people and in front of local and international public opinion at the time, like as: the mayors, leaders of the Baath Party, directors of departments, factories, companies and members of the Parliament, they were all models and fake pictures, they are chosen, appointed and even fake elections were fabricated for them, then they are placed in the places that were chosen for them, by the authority of the intelligence branch. These alleged officials remain subject to the intelligence orders, and who thinks of the rebellion among them, he is removed immediately in various ways, and the intelligence put others at his place, of course, these people are not chosen for the positions of responsibility by the intelligence according to their qualifications, their good conduct, their morals or their popularity, quite the opposite, the corrupt, pimps, alcoholics, and gay pedophile people were the closest and the most valuable persons to the corrupt intelligence officers and leaders who love spreading corruption, and they are preferred to be nominated for all positions, because these people have no political ambitions, but their biggest and only concern is to satisfy their desires and whims, and they never mind participating in any corruption on their way to satisfy their whims.

As for the honorable and religious people who were still working in state jobs, they have always been chased, monitored and isolated, because their presence breaks and obstructs the closed circle of corruption and bribery networks. Therefore, they were disposed of as soon as possible, in any way, even if it was by fabricating any accusation against them, that might lead them to lose their life and future. There are so many examples, I knew them in details, about the Assad regime's intending to choose scum people to appoint them in important and sensitive positions and jobs, it seemed like a kind of black comedy because of how absurd this model of people is, and their incompatibility with the work assigned to them, really, they differed with the qualities needed in humorously, and it is deplorable because of the tragedy and dire situation that the Syrian people have been living in, and the degree of injustice that make them to be silent about these farces, for example, the position of Director of the Islamic Endowments Directorate in Hama, which is assumed to be a very sensitive and extremely important job for the vast majority of the Syrian people, because it relates to the management and organization of mosques and legal institutes, the appointment and transfer of sheikhs and scholars, and overseeing Islamic charitable projects ... etc. In all countries of the world where there are such types of directorates, the director must be chosen according to his good reputation and character, and he must be religiously committed to fit the requirements of this job, but the Assad regime had maliciously and deliberately appointed someone called Ghalib as a director of the Endowments of Hama, he is alcoholic, corrupted, bribed, a thief, and his reputation is very bad also, and he still had this job for many years, so that the workers and employees of the

Intelligence Branch mentioned this matter in their conversations every time, with laughed and gloats, because they considered it as another dirty achievement that they succeeded in. Also, I remember something related to this, that, after few years, I was investigating intelligence issues related to corruption and bribery in some trade unions in Hama, and I was surprised when I checked the biography of one of the leaders of these unions, which was a large and important union, that he was previously known to have done homosexual blackmail and was involved in obscene acts, and his reputation is poor! At first, I was surprised how this happened, in a small city like Hama, almost all of its residents know each other, how was this corrupt person elected to this place by his union workers !?, moreover, when I started studying the biography of a second union leader, I was more surprised by the fact that his abnormal tendencies and his bad reputation matched with those of the first one, actually, I thought maybe it was just a strange coincidence !! but when the biography of a third union leader resembled the previous two in everything, I was completely shocked and knew it was definitely not a coincidence, and I became very curious to know the secret of this matter, and who is supporting it!?

After efforts and researches, I finally knew, that after the Hama events in 1982, a person was appointed as the head of the Workers' Union in Hama, according to an order of the Military Intelligence Branch there; although it is legally presumed to be elected by the workers. This man was a well-known pimp, and the people in Hama know that he was also an alcohol addicted person and deals with all sins, among them was his love to sexual abuse. He was appointed to this work because he was the obedient servant of the intelligence officers, their detective, and one of their spies on Hama's citizens, so he became responsible of selecting and appointing trade union managers, of course, he chose those who were like him and who shared him moral dirt. Assad regime criminals were in agreement and happy with this choice.

My training with Suhail in Hama lasted several months, then I was sent with several other officers, so that, every time, I be with one of them until knowing his work sector, then I turn to another, until the end of this period, I became to know most of the city's neighborhoods and most of its factories, institutions and banks. The news began to spread quickly in Hama, among the employees, and among ordinary people about my presence as a new Sunni Muslim employee in the Military Intelligence branch, of course, it was the first time, that they would see or hear about a person in this place of work, who was a city resident, especially from Homs, the nearest city to them, and they were more surprised when they know how much the work, that assigned to me within the branch, was sensitive and important, it is the economic sector, which was usually given only to the close Nusayri officers who were supported by the leaders of the regime.

However, it is good to mention, for those who do not know the details of the Syrian sectarian situation under the rule of Assad, that one of the funny and strange things that made everyone surprised, either within the intelligence system or among the civilian people, when they hear or know about my presence in the intelligence work throughout these many years that I spent in my work with the Syrian intelligence and army, in addition to all the reasons and things that I mentioned and explained earlier, It is the title which I hold

!!! Whereas, since my early youth, and as a result of my great love and admiration for the biography of the famous companion of our master Muhammad, (the Messenger of Allah peace be upon him), Omar bin Al-Khattab - may Allah bless him - I had called myself "Abo Omar". And according to the customs and traditions that prevailed in our society and cities, we use nicknames more than names, so everyone knew me and addressed me with this name, but what is the problem or strangeness in this!?

Most Syrians know that it is among the beliefs of the ruling Nusayri sect in Syria that they imitate the Shiites in some matters, the most important of it, that they hate the Companions of the Prophet, peace and blessings be upon him, they insult them, always talk about them badly, and they consider these actions and sayings against the Companions, as one of their religious duties, particularly, the two greatest and most famous companions, Abu Bakr Al-Siddiq and Omar Bin Al-Khattab, may God be pleased with them.

In Syria, after this sect managed to dominate everything, they intended to increase and announce these abusive sayings and insults everywhere and every time in defiance and humiliation of the Sunni majority. For this reason, all Syrians generally avoided calling themselves or their children by names or titles that included the names of these Companions, so that the regime's executioners do not consider them enemies, in order not to attract the hostility of the Assad sect, which is provoked by these names, then they are subjected to obstructing their life matters, harm or even death at any moment by one of the servants of this regime. Whereas within the military and intelligence services, these names were completely non-existent, because the rare minority of

Sunni Muslims working in these services, it was never in their interest to challenge their masters and leaders with names and surnames that bother them, so imagine the tragic situation and the amount of injustice that millions of Sunni Muslims lived with in Syria for more than forty years, whereas, they were afraid and could not even give the name that they loved for themselves or their children, because of their fear of the oppression and retaliation from this regime, which could get them under the pretext of this simple matter, which is very normal for people in other countries that lead a normal life.

Because of this all, I were, thanks to Allah, since I volunteered for this job at the end of 1993 until the date of my arrest by the Assad son's (Bashar) regime in 2012 and years after, the only person with the name "Abo Omar" among all the different Syrian army, security, and intelligence forces. So that my friends and I have been reassuring every period of time of being alone on that, and betting on it out of curiosity or banter sometimes, also, I always challenged everyone to find someone else with this name who works in the intelligence or the army. And every time, the result is the same, no one, and this name and my boldness to carry it while I was living among the enemies was a surprise to everyone who heard it during my life, whether of the Nusayris I have been meeting in the branch or other intelligence and military locations, or of the ordinary citizens of other denominations, and they were talking about this issue among themselves as strange news, I often heard someone whispering or chatting with someone else on the phone, or sometimes someone tells me that he heard one of them say to the other: Did you know that in the Hama

Intelligence branch there is a person who calls himself "Abo Omar" !!?

I always said to myself, and to whom I trust, through the years, and I still say that I ask Allah to be pleased with me, and to accept what I have done over the years, challenging these unjust criminals in everything, even in the name that I chose for myself, although I spent my life between them and their own home and their regime.

At the end of 1995, after about six months of field training, I was made responsible for an intelligence work sector made up of a number of factories, institutions and companies, then I became formally responsible to the Military Intelligence Branch leadership for the follow-up and monitoring of the work progress in this sector, and to report immediately any defect or problem in it at any time. The cars of these factories and companies were put in my service, and I could bring any of it with a driver during my work, and to use it on my transfers as I wish at any time.

My first years at work in the branch were years of founding, learning and getting to know everything, moreover, working hours were very long, and the work was very exhausting, especially with the need to coexist with such models of degraded human scum beings like the officers who work with me in the intelligence branch, and who were always proud of their actions, that any ordinary person with little morals should be ashamed of mentioning. Usually, the daily work program started from early morning with writing reports and intelligence issues in the office at the branch's headquarters, then receiving the tasks that must be done, and meeting the leaders if it is necessary, then each of us communicates by phone with the sector in which he works, such as factories and companies, and he asks them to send any cars available. After that, each officer goes to patrol the offices, divisions, and warehouses of every company or factory that he is being charged with controlling; he interviews dozens of managers, employees, engineers, and ordinary workers every day, he investigates with them, and continues to follow the work of dozens of them, this work is repeated until the end of the official working time, when all officers return to the headquarters of the branch. After that, each officer is assigned to do patrols that will continue for long hours, wandering and watching the streets and neighborhoods of the city, then, at night, we usually patrolled hotels and nightclubs in Hama and its countryside, where we roam in those places to monitor and check the names and personalities of its users, customers and visitors. This work continues until the next morning, when we go back without getting any sleep or rest to follow our sectors of government departments again until noon, and then finally comes the time to leave work to rest in our homes for only twelve hours, then we return the next morning to repeat the same daily routine mentioned.

And of course, in addition to all usual everyday work, which I have explained, there are a lot of additional intelligence works that arises suddenly too often, like house raids, and monitoring and hunting down fugitives wanted persons or some smugglers. In brief, the system of work of the Military Intelligence Branch in Hama was thirty-six hours of work, then only twelve hours rest, of course, it is a very tiring system, and it was not the same in all other intelligence branches in Syria; The reason for this is that, despite the Assad regime's crushing of Hama and its residents, they believed that it was still the most dangerous place which threats the existence of this regime, therefore, they put the Military Intelligence branch in a state of constant alert for many years. As a result of this exhausting and permanent work, in addition to the spiritual emptiness and moral corruption they have, and despite the many and big financial gains that officers and the workers/employees of the branch were getting from their corruption and blackmailing people, there were cases of mental and psychological illness among officers and employees of the branch that happened every period, and I saw many of it by myself, like one time as a Nusayri officer, his nickname was /Bosso/, in the first days of my work in the branch, and after depression, he committed suicide by shooting himself inside the branch, and another officer, named Asif, who had a critical and sensitive job in the branch, suffered a madness that he never recovered from, and another named Bassam Mansour, he is from the Nusayri villages of Masyaf, suffered from severe depression, that made him silent for years.

From the first important things that I have seen, and knew about many of its hidden details, at my early years in the Military Intelligence branch in Hama, are the famous events of February 1982, but my knowledge of the secrets of these events was completely different from all other people, because I may be the only person in the world, and because of the nature of my work, who heard the testimonies of both sides, the murderer and the murdered, the torturer and the victim, and the unjust criminal regime and oppressed people, in addition, of course, to viewing the files and the very classified intelligence studies, that made the picture complete in my mind about what happened in the 1982 Hama massacre, the old Nusayri officers of intelligence, who participated in the crimes that took place in the city, in many times - after several drinking of fine and expensive liquor, that they got as daily bribes from nightclubs, illegal bars, or some smugglers; after they get drunk, during some night sessions in working shifts within branch offices, they start chatting, boasting, and remembering the disgusting crimes they did or participated in in Hama during and after the events of the Muslim Brotherhood, and they talked with a laugh, as if they were talking about bravery, for example, they told me how they once did a race and a bet on who among them could hit a huge minaret of one of Hama's mosques, in a neighborhood called Al-Bayyad, by the portable missile launchers, and made it collapsing on the mosque, and how they finally succeeded, after several direct hits, until it finally collapsed over the mosque and the people inside, moreover, they mentioned how much they laughed at the cries of pain and terror that they heard from the worshipers and the people who were inside the mosque when it collapsed, when some were killed and others were injured. They also enjoyed a lot, when they remembered how a group of them lighted fire in Islamic scientists' beards, then enjoyed watching their pain before they killed them, and how an officer called Musa did uproot the beard of a well-known cleric in Hama using a metal pliers, this cleric is from a famous family /from Al-Jajah family/.

And as for their favorite stories, which they always loved to repeat at that time, were the stories of rape and sexual harassment of citizens, where they talked in front of me again and again and in detail, how a Nusayri intelligence officer named /Muhammad Al-Hassan "Abo Amer"/ raped the wife of a great and famous scientist of Islamic sciences in Hama (I will not mention his name, respecting him and his family and their privacy) along with a group of other officers at gunpoint during their raid and inspection of his home. And they assured me that /Abo Amer/ likes to rape the wives of sheikhs and Islamic sciences scientists particularly, and he was repeating this act on other women, whenever the opportunity arose to him. This officer, Abo Amer, who was still working with us in the economic office in the branch at the time, he was a short, slim-bodied man, ugly looking, and always smelly. When his story was told by others with his presence, he exploded laughing, pleased and proud of it.

Once, they also mentioned that another officer of the branch, and while they broke into one of the civilians' homes in Hama, he pulled one of the women to a nearby apartment, meanwhile, he was carrying a Kalashnikov rifle and threatening her, then he tore her clothes off, and raped her by force; she was shouting and begging everybody, she was saying: Please, I am married, please leave me, because I am pregnant, but, the officer continued carelessly without any interest in her cries and begging, while the other officers, who were with him on this mission, were listening to everything and laughing. In the branch when they told this last criminal story to me or someone of them, they were imitating the movements of that officer while he was raping and holding the rifle attached to his shoulder with his hand, and they imitated the cry of the poor victim, and were laughing with joy.

From the stories that I heard from them also, is one that is exactly identical with what the civilians of Hama told me, those who witnessed its events, It was about the Kilaniya neighborhood which was a major and famous neighborhood in Hama, that some of its residents -who are all from the same family /the Kilani family/ - were among the richest and wealthiest of Hama people, and how the officers of the Syrian army that is led by the Assad regime along with the intelligence officers, during the destruction of this neighborhood, collected all adult women and young girls they found in this neighborhood from their homes, and kept them in a nearby house, that the officers had made a temporary headquarter for them, then, for days, they brutally raped all detained women, taking turns on that. After that, the fate of these women and underage girls was not known, but both intelligence agents and the Hama citizens have told this story to me at different times and occasions, and they also added, that there were witnesses from both sides, shortly after those terrible events, that saw traces of blood and a large amount of women's underwear and outer garments contaminated with these blood in the house where the army officers were stationed. Moreover, all the officers of the Military Intelligence Branch always repeated in their conversations with each other, the revolting phrase or what they considered as an example for others and they recommended each other by it:

"Who didn't try the taste of raping Hama city girls, - they mean Sunni Muslim ones of course -, whatever he does, it will be like he has never tasted real women in his life!!".

Rape and sexual assaults, by intelligence officers and employees of the Military Intelligence Branch in Hama, were not taking place using weapons and violence only, but I could hear other things that were happening earlier; and thereafter, I saw cases like those of blackmail, threats and psychological pressure which were applied on females in Hama for a period of more than a quarter of a century, Whereas, in all the offices of the leadership of the intelligence branches and senior officers, there were hidden internal rooms always equipped for these attacks, when the women, from most of the families from Hama, were brought by force and threat to the branch headquarters every day, then, they are left for long hours, and sometimes from early morning until late at night, confined in closed rooms and in uncomfortable conditions, some of them are accompanied by children or babies, too, and this compulsory invitation is repeated for days, sometimes for weeks, until they reach a severe state of collapse, despair and fear, then they are taken to the officers' interview who begin to blackmail them in order to financially or sexually exploit them, by threatening the mentioned women and girls and making them scared of facing deadly charges from the intelligence system against them or their husbands, and families, and this pressure and blackmail continues for these women and girls until they agree to pay the price for their deliverance from this calamity and those threats, either by their bodies if they have a beauty that the criminals of the branch desire and that girls agree on this choice because of despair, fatigue and fear, or by paying large sums of cash as bribes for officers and intelligence personnel to get rid of this torture. I have been watching such miserable women daily for sixteen years during my work in the Military Intelligence branch in Hama, they come in the morning to the headquarters of the branch when I leave to work in the city, then I see them leaving the place at night when I return. The more the woman resists and refuses to obey the wishes of the criminals and keeps defending her honor, the longer the period of torture and extortion by intelligence criminals will be.

As for what I heard from the Hama city's civilians, it was a lot. They who lived the tragedy and witnessed the Hama massacre in 1982, their fear for their children made them remain silent long despite their wounds, pains, worries and oppression that they faced and that are greater and more than what a person can bear, but little by little - thanks to Allah – and year after year (and after they made sure that I am completely different from the rest of the intelligence personnel, and that I am not their enemy, but I am one of them, and I do not differ from them) they managed to break the wall of fear with me, and they regained the confidence and hope that among these dirty human demons, can be found - thanks to Allah - someone who tries his best to help and protect them. Their stories of what they experienced were making the heart cry before the eye, about children killed in cold blood in front of their parents, about a father who was stabbed, then he was shot in front of his wife and children, and on how the army, the intelligence, and the armed sectarian civilians -those were brought from the Nusayri villages surrounding Hama - collected the families from the homes, women, men and children, then lined them up against the walls of the buildings and opened fire with machine guns at them all. And the thing that seems like a kind of black comedy and is disgusting too is, as many people from Hama told me and assured me, that the only person from Hama who could have powers and permission from Assad Regime's crime officers, during that terrible time, to save people from being killed or executed - even if it was in the last moments, after putting them in the final death line up to kill them - this person is the most famous pimp and prostitute known in Hama at that time, she is called Um Samir, and because of what she was personally providing, and those working for her, / It is a narration and witness also confirmed to me by some Nusayri intelligence personnel too/, she could, if she made one signal to the soldiers or the executioner or one of the criminals during that criminality events save the people she chose,/and she often chose them because they are similar to her in dirtiness and the low level of morality or they are some of her clients/, from certain death.

Also, the people of Hama told me how the Assad regime and its criminals randomly killed without cause, without charge or trial, where the killing was just for killing, and genocide or extermination on sectarian basis only, the bodies were collected every day by bulldozers and heavy machinery in piles rising many meters in the air, and all of them are unarmed civilians, because all who were originally armed all over the city of Hama, and tried to defend themselves, their number wasn't more than hundreds, and with light individual weapons.

This are the accurate and correct information that I obtained through my audit of thousands of dossiers, studies and files during my years of work, and through the testimonies that I heard from those who were present from both sides, the side of the killers and the side of families of the victims. Because of the hundreds fighters that were in Hama at that time, and under the pretext of their existence, the regime brought tens of thousands of armed murderer criminals, in addition to cannons, planes, armored vehicles, and heavy weapons, to slaughter tens of thousands of innocent people, and arresting an equal number almost, most of them were minors, and destroying an entire city over its population and while they were inside it, furthermore, to persecute, spread injustice, and repress millions of people for decades throughout Syria.

During my first years in my field work, I began more and more and through the meeting and hearing and control of thousands of male and female workers and employees (who work within the sector that I was responsible on), I began to form, in my mind, a complete understanding of the city of Hama and its families and their way of life and dealings; although I am from a neighboring city, however, each region and city has matters that set it apart and give it its own character. In fact, in the beginning, it was never easy for me, because it took too long by the people of Hama to be able to break the wall of hidden fear and hatred that they feel against any intelligence employee, but after a while, they began to secretly transfer and share my name among them, and watch my behavior silently, they were surprised /from my presence among the intelligence officers/ like the others were.

It was usual, as all workers and those who are familiar with this systems know how the intelligence services work in all countries of the world and of course, Syria is one of them, that the security and intelligence services rely in obtaining and collecting information on a number of ways and sources, the most important one of them was the so-called /informants/, those who are ordinary civilian citizens living among us like other people, but they secretly spy, follow-up and record what is happening around them in their community and workplaces, and sometimes even within their families, then transfer it in detail to the officers, intelligence employees and personnel whose assigned them to this work, this is in exchange for support, material gains, protection or other personal interests that the informant wishes to obtain from the intelligence system. The intelligence officer or employee can never succeed in his work without a network of informers that works for providing him with this information. We call this intelligence term / the source or sources of information /. And whenever the network of informants and sources expands in number and effectiveness, the information of the officer or employee who manages and deals with them become stronger and more abundant.

As a result of the fact that the Assad regime depends only on the dirty and corrupt kind of intelligence officers and employees, so were the informants and the sources of the intelligence systems all the same type and degraded level. Regarding to that, the only people who cooperate with the Syrian intelligence or provide information to them are:

Firstly - The Nusayris, that are of course a part of the sectarian system, but they could not provide the necessary information because they cannot know anything about what is going on among the citizens of all other sects in Syria, especially the Sunni majority, because everyone knew that the members of the Nusayri sect were an integral part of their system; so, the members of other sects in Syria were avoiding mixing with them, moreover, they hide everything from them, and they stay always in complete attention and beware of them.

Secondly – bad eccentrics, corrupts and outcasts among the Sunnis Muslims /and there are in every community bad people like those who basically own a bad reputation/, because these kinds of persons have nothing to lose if people pay attention to them and revealed their dealings with criminals of the intelligence service, of course, this type of human being has no moral or religious deterrent that can prevent any normal person from dealing with such a nasty system.

Because of this, all Hama Intelligence Branch informants and sources were alcoholics, pimps, prostitutes, thieves, embezzlers, venal persons, suspects and former perpetrators of crimes, persons who are addicted to visiting degenerated bars and nightclubs, and homosexual exploiters, all of those were - in cooperation with Assad intelligence personnel of course- working different than all other intelligence services in the world, and in a way that is in opposition to good moral reasoning, they were supporting and protecting the corrupt and the bad people, and helping them, they even nominate them for sensitive positions and jobs, and help them to reach them, while they consider the others who are honest and loyal in their jobs and who are committed to morality and religion to be their enemies, and as the main obstacle in their way to enjoy their filth. Therefore, they were waiting for them, for any slip of tongue or behavior to fabricate ready-made charges against them, such as accusation of hostility toward the regime or to the Ba'ath party, and the charge of sympathy for the Muslim Brotherhood, and other charges to get rid of them and remove them from their path. The intelligence leaders and Assad regime leaders were pleased with this of course, and always encouraged it, because they were relying on spreading corruption in the Syrian society as one of the methods that weakens this society, as this will help them take more control of Syria.

In fact, my first struggle - during my first years in Hama - was with myself!

Yes, it was with myself, because the power, strength, and authority I gained as a young man at the time - while most of my peers were still just college students - were very tempting, these powers had a charm, and it cannot easily be resisted, because everything in the world that anyone desires or wishes for or seeks it and what people spend their efforts and money to get it, was available in front of me, free, in large amounts, and in daily basis. All the managers of companies and factories could not refuse any request from me or from any military intelligence officer, some of them were afraid of the oppression of the unjust regime against them or against their family, and others were partners in corruption and thefts with the regime, and they want to preserve their earnings; while some of them were previously put in office by the intelligence services and on their orders, because they work as informants and spy to them against the people. Whoever was trying to rebel against or oppose the Military Intelligence Authority, or leans with another intelligence authority, immediately he and his family and everyone who has any value to him, had been put under the intelligence microscope, until one of them fell into any mistake or slip of the tongue.

Because the Military Intelligence Service System in Syria among other intelligence services was the only one in charge of monitoring and spying on all landline telephone calls (which was the only way to communicate in Syria at that time), so it was exploiting this in a worst way in subjecting people by revealing their secrets, where our branch's officers knew through the recorded daily phone calls, secrets about families even some members of these families don't know it, for example, we knew who secretly cheats on his wife, with whom, and where, and of woman who cheats on her husband, without anyone knowing it, in details, and the girl or young man who are having an illegal relationship, and many other secrets of people and homes. The officers and intelligence personnel took advantage of these secrets in the most heinous manner in blackmailing people, especially the rich ones, for their money, and sometimes for their honor and women.

   I remember one of the incidents that were famous in Hama similar to this exploiting cases, it is that one senior official in the Hama directorate of Agriculture during this period, who, because of his relationship to one of the officials close to the leaders of the Assad regime in Damascus, tried to rebel against the authority of the Military Intelligence Branch over him and his directorate, and refused to obey the orders of the branch's chief and officers and their interference in his work, so he and all his family were put under constant surveillance, until they discovered - by monitoring the phone of his home - that his wife was cheating on him, by making sexual relations with one of her husband's drivers, who was with a car from the agriculture directorate specified in serving the manager's house, this wife always complained to this driver about impotence that her husband suffers from, during her phone calls with him, then, the Military Intelligence branch monitored the wife and driver until they were caught while committing the scandal, then they were taken completely naked to the headquarters of the branch, and the husband -the director and manager of agriculture who knew nothing about all this topic- was brought to the branch headquarters, and his wife and his driver were showed to him as they were in a disgraceful view, then the officers bargained with this manager, either he and his children get exposed, and the news of this matter will be published in all parts of the city of Hama, or this manager will acquiesce to the branch completely, in exchange for not publishing this news. Of course, he chose the total obedience to the branch, to preserve his honor and that of his children.

I also remember another such incident, when the governor of Hama was subjugated; who was at the time an engineer from the countryside of Damascus, then, he thought that his position as governor would protect him from the influence and domination of military intelligence on everything, and he tried not to obey them, so the branch exploited the secret relationship that it revealed, between him and a notorious woman -she was a member of the leadership of the Baath Party branch in Hama-, through the phone calls that were recorded between them, to set pressure on him firstly, then get rid of him afterwards.

Because of these and other methods, no manager or department head in any factory or company could refuse any request from me or any other military intelligence officer, and all the cars and drivers of government departments were put at my disposal and in my service. Every day, many of the employees in these departments, especially the corrupt ones ,offered all the temptations they could for me, they always tried to give me gifts, bribes, banquets and invitations to homes and luxury restaurants, even the girls were being offered to me. But the good education I had in my family before and the religious and moral background I had, had the greatest impact on my ability to win over myself and my desires, and not to accept these multiple temptations. However, the more I reject these offers and the temptations, two important things were happening:

The first was the increasing hatred of many corrupt people against me, those who were close to the old intelligence staff and the increasing of their desire to get rid of me and conspire against me more.

The second was the spread of my name and reputation and what I was doing secretly among the honest and oppressed in Hama, until most of the people of Hama had heard and knew of my presence in the Hama Intelligence Branch, consequently, I became famous and my story spread among them.

I needed several years at the beginning of my field work in Hama until I was able to gradually build and establish mutual trust with types of humans, which are quite different from the types that other intelligence officers relied on for getting information, and I managed -because of the help and blessing of Allah first, and secondly because of my honesty with people - to build a large network of friends and acquaintances in Hama, whether they are ordinary civilians working in trade and handicrafts, or from the directors of the departments, engineers and employees in the departments and government factories.

Since the corruption current in the intelligence system was strong, I needed two things to resist this current: the first is to make my own small countercurrent, this is what happened through the responsiveness and cooperation of many honest citizens and employees of Hama with me; the second is to ensure support and protection to me from the fierce war that began against me by all other officers and intelligence employees, when they started to notice, years later, that I broke the networks of corruption that they were mired in for years; and I was surprised that protection was provided to me in a strong and continuous way for many years, from where I did not expect; how did this happen?

In the Assad era in all state organs, including the security and intelligence services, there were always a clandestine or sometimes open conflict between officers and officials over everything, conflicts to get closer to the top leaders, for power and influence, on thefts, bribes and other gains that can be obtained.

In Hama's branch of military intelligence, like other branches, these conflicts were always inflaming and happening, especially among commanding officers, and in the first years when I started working in the Hama branch, the main and biggest conflict was between the head of the branch Brigadier General Ahmad Halloum, and the deputy head of the branch and head of information Section Colonel Mohammed al-Sha'ar. And the rest of the officers in the branch, were inclined at each time to one of the two mentioned, according to their personal interests and ambitions. From my early months in this branch, and after I knew about this conflict, I decided that one of my most important tasks that I should always strive to do is the incitement to more of these conflicts and to create a strife among all the criminals who surround me in this work; I was not limited in this work to officers or the Military Intelligence Branch, but throughout my work there, I was able to widen the circle of differences among our branch officers and even among the other intelligence branches officers, I even succeeded, thanks to Allah, in expelling criminal officers and saving people in Hama from their evil, the highest rank was a Brigadier General in the state intelligence system called Ali

Yunus, who was the head of the state intelligence branch in Hama, the reports that I wrote against him, in addition to following him, monitoring him, and inciting the head of the Military Intelligence Branch against him, were the causes behind transferring him from Hama, after he had exhausted the people in this city with hurting them and blackmailing them. So, how were these conflicts a reason to protect me!?

After a while, and after I started providing the branch with a lot of reports and intelligence topics about corruption that I almost found everywhere and in every office of the establishments and factories that I was responsible for (the bribery, embezzlement, thefts, and patronage were being dealt with daily in government sectors), and they were always overlooked on purpose by other officers and intelligence employees, after they get paid for it; I started raising these topics and not accepting any price for my silence.

I expected, and everyone who knew what I was doing, that I will not stay at this work long before they get rid of me, by moving me to any other job or maybe even in a way that is even worse than that. But Allah - the Almighty – has willed that these conflicts become a reason that made Colonel Mohammed al-Sha'ar -my department chief - very pleased with these topics that I detected and raised, not because of a sincerity at work or that he liked me, and not because his target was to hold the corrupt whom I report in my intelligence reports accountable, but he knew by his guile, slyness, and experience that what I do would serve his interests in many ways: First, the intensity of my work in pursuing corruption, and the reputation of this work that spread among the people, will strengthen his status, fame, authority and influence as an intelligence officer, whether among intelligence leaders or civilians, because he is my chief, and he always sends the very important subjects I discovered to the capital in his own name, there were among them sometimes topics of embezzlement of tens of millions of state funds at the time, and this helped him improving his image in front of senior leaders, and to cover up other topics that he have received large amounts of money to be silence about. Secondly, when I was putting pressure on the corrupt and pursuing them, this would make them invoke officials and officers who were participating and supporting them in their businesses, and they ask them to mediate with Colonel Mohammed to stop and hide my reports against them at any costs, this was also supporting Colonel Mohammed's business and was bringing benefits to him, because he expands his circle of knowledge and influence. The third of these benefits to Colonel Mohammed from my work are the cash and the precious gifts which he was receiving from many persons to cover up their dirty work that I uncovered through my work, and I brought the evidence and the relevant documents about them to the branch.

And in order to preserve all these advantages, which I later understood and became sure of gradually, when my experience increased, Colonel Mohammed put all his power and influence to keep me continuing what I was doing, and this surprised me at first, then I understood its causes over time. Despite my knowledge of the fate of my topics and my efforts, and that the corruption I uncover will not often be combated, I never had any other choice within my limited capabilities in this intelligence service, because my work in the intelligence against corrupt persons, embezzlers and thieves, was better than -God forbid- if I had to hurt people as other officers do, even if these corrupt people were often not held accountable. But at least that was showing me to the rest of the intelligence branch officers as a productive intelligence officer, this also justified the usefulness of my presence in this branch, and most importantly of all it provided me with a good cover for the real work I was doing in secret.

During my long years of working in the Military Intelligence Branch in Hama, there were dozens of attempts to hurt me and get rid of me by Nusayri officers, employees and agents in the branch, these attempts were repeated every period of time; moreover, in every time, they were trying to make bigger and more serious charges against me, accompanied by testimonies of thieves and corrupt civilians who are also very interested in getting rid of me. But, because of my good reputation as someone with clean hands which is known to everyone and none of them can deny it, so these charges were not related to the financial and economic affairs that I work for, but they were trying to accuse me once of persecuting religious minorities, ridiculing of other religions, or persecuting employees and dealing with them cruelly. But every time, Colonel Mohammed al-Sha'ar stopped the proceedings against me then told me about it, so Allah -the Almighty- sent and guided this man to protect me from where I do not expect, praise and thanks to Allah always and forever.

The days and years were passing while I was in this work, and although my hatred toward my enemies from the Assad regime was increasing day by day and year after year the more I knew them, but I was pleased and comfortable with what I had accomplished so far, and what I was still doing, of the goals and actions that I have borne all these efforts and spent all these years for. I was always keeping short copies of any important intelligence topic I work on, especially if it contains information that could be useful in the future in condemning the Assad regime, or any one of his senior officers in their crimes against the Syrian people, if he will be held accountable one day. I was writing this information on notebooks and papers on the pretext that it is a draft of my intelligence reports and will be destroyed later, but in fact, I always moved them to a safe secret hideout in my home in Homs.

One of the missions that I succeeded to accomplish, and which I ask Allah to accept it from me, is that every once in a while, I succeeded in saving the lives of a number of oppressed men and women, those who would have been arrested for mere words of criticism about the Assad regime or one of his officials, or because one of them performed some prayers and worships, so they accused him unfairly that he sympathizes with the Muslim Brotherhood, and other ridiculous charges, which were enough, in Syria under the Assad regime, to arrest and eliminate people without anybody to watch or judge the criminal officers. I was sometimes managing to hide the reports against these innocent people, when it was in my hands, for periods of time until I was absolutely sure they were forgotten, then I destroyed them after that, and sometimes I acquitted them of the charges if I was in charge of the inspection and interrogation with them. And in many other times, I absolutely refrained from delivering this type of reports to the branch, or to inform anyone about it when some dirty informants delivered it to me.

When I knew that someone would be arrested because of these false charges, or because of a personal or telephone surveillance process against him to prepare for his arrest, I was trying to leak the news to this person, or to a relative or acquaintance of his indirectly, through methods that vary in each case, so that he can take care and pay attention and escape before falling into the hands of the intelligence branch. And during my time among employees, factories workers and companies, I always tried to help the oppressed, vulnerable and religiously committed persons. On the other hand, obstructing the affairs of those supported by the regime and its agents and officials, who are the scum of people and they are from the evilest of them usually.

My reputation and actions have become known to both sides in my work sector and in the city of Hama in general, thus attempts to tempt me with money from the affected people from among the corrupted were frequent more and more, and each time they increased the amount offered to me more. I remember that the general manager of the Hama Cement Company, which is a company comprised of several factories, and I was for a long time as an intelligence officer responsible for watching and controlling everything there, he said to me once when we were talking:

You made everyone tired because of you -he means of course the corrupted people-, O "Abo Omar"; I said: Why!?

He replied: because all the security and intelligence officers whose we knew previously, we could know what is their price after a while; but you, despite the multiplicity and diversity of material and moral offers or social benefits and their magnitude, despite that years have passed, no one could find your price!

This was a testimony -thanks to Allah- from him and others to me, that I was hearing at various times during my working years in Hama; It was assuring me that I was still on the right track

Within the headquarters of the branch, and during the times I was spending among the officers, I succeeded in creating chaos and inaction among them. I always encouraged them to escape during missions, patrols, and guard shifts. My only Sunni Muslim colleague in the branch Haitham -who I mentioned earlier – was noticing these things and actions from me, because after years I have trusted him, and we were always spending most of the time together, so he was noticing me without knowing the real reasons of my actions; and he thought it was only because of feelings of hate that we all have as a Sunni majority for these foolish enemies; who are also enemies of our homeland, as a result of their atrocities against the Syrian people.

It was one of the most important things that I succeeded in completing, in terms of incitement to inaction, is the issue of prayer and Friday speech, when all the branches of security and intelligence of various kinds in Syria monitor the mosques, prayer, and the single prayers permanently, as I explained earlier, and because everybody know that Friday prayers are the most important collective Islamic prayer every week, which is held in all mosques in Syria without exception, and usually attended by more worshipers than any other prayer, for this reason, all branches of the Syrian intelligence services send officers and agents of each branch to every mosque throughout Syria, the task of this officers was to watch the worshipers, the khatib (the Islamic scientists who speak and give Friday religion lessons), and the Imam, and to spy on their actions and sayings, and so as to inform it to the branch where he works later, and write it down in a written report. Since the Assad regime control of Syria, he made a new intelligence law among many of the repressive laws, it is forcing all khatibs (I explained to you the meaning of this Islamic name before) of mosques in Syria to read unified Friday speeches, that were written by the regime and prepared for them in the intelligence authorities, then distributed to those khatibs, whereas its content is always about glorifying Assad, his rule, his party, his policies and all his actions. Thus, the regime turned Friday speeches from religious to silly political speeches under pressure and threats.

Because of this, one of the main tasks that we were all assigned as intelligence officers when we carry out the task of observing Friday prayers, was checking the khatib's commitment to the compulsory speech that was given to him, and that he didn't go off topic, or add to it any other topic, with attention to him if he reduces any words that praise the criminal Hafez al-Assad. If the khatib of the mosque made any violation of what I mentioned, the intelligence employee who is responsible for the observation immediately informs the branch he works for, then this khatib is summoned to a group of insults and threats in the branch, Its severity and results increase or decrease depending on the amount of offense and the disobeying he has committed, and the level of criminality of the executioners of the branch who work on his subject. This situation has always created to me severe psychological distress and discomfort, that's when I saw the respected Islamic scientists in Hama - mostly elderly - humiliated and insulted by scum people in my branch, because of simple words they added or decreased in their Friday speech in the mosque. So I worked very hard during my years of work to incite officers of the Military Intelligence Branch in Hama to escape and not to carry out the task of observing Friday speeches; and convinced them that it was a ridiculous task, and that there is no khatib who dares to disobey the orders and instructions, Moreover, I was offering them invitations every Friday to eat at my own expense, to attend movies in cinemas, or for a hike in a park, and each time for a different new set of branch officers. That was because of my knowledge about their greed and love for any gain of any kind, in order to distract them from the task of Friday, and accustom them to neglecting it. Thanks to Allah, after many years of efforts on this subject, I managed to change things completely in the Military Intelligence Branch in Hama, after all the officers in this branch were committed to the task of monitoring mosques on Friday, the opposite has become true, where in my last years in the branch, the situation has arrived that only a very small number of officers were still committed to this task, these actions were a reason to relieve Hama people of the harm or cancel it in some cases, and perhaps to save some lives thanks to Allah Almighty.

Finally, The Tyrant died...
But after he had killed many people and damaged something inside all the others!

In the first months of the year 2000, and one day, after I had spent whole years in this job, exactly I had been working in the Military Intelligence Branch in Hama for six years that day ,and during a meeting for the officers of the information department and the head of the department Colonel Mohammed Al-Sha'ar, I was surprised when he informed me and announced to everybody else with us in the meeting, that I was awarded the Order of Merit from Syria's greatest criminal, President Hafez al-Assad, It was the highest order usually given to intelligence personnel, and I was told that the reason of that was due to the heavy economic intelligence reports that I provided to the branch throughout my work, and because of the importance of the topics which were contained in all these reports. The branch of Hama was officially notified of this and it was registered in my official file, really it was an amazing surprise for me, because from the first moment I entered this field, and started working in the intelligence of Assad regime, I was expecting to be arrested at any moment or even to be assassinated, in case of discovering: my political background against them, what I was planning against them before, what I sabotaged and leaked of information and intelligence data, or even to get rid of my permanent disturbances to some officers in the branch as I discovered their partners, their agents, their corrupt informants, thieves and bribes. But I didn't expect any honors, and I never thought that honoring would come on behalf of the greatest criminal who is the worst one of my own enemies and those of my country and people, It seemed to me as a comic thing, that they thank me for something if they knew it truly, and who am I in truth, they would execute me immediately.

But, after my surprise disappeared, I was really very pleased and proud of myself, not because this human demon, Hafez al-Assad, and his dirty criminal men honored me, as the honoring from these people to anyone is usually considered -for me and for the most of the Syrian people- unacceptable and a crime certificate according to my principles and what I have learned from morality and religion, but my pleasure and pride was because I discovered how much God's help and care made me successful in penetrating and deceiving these fools and in manipulating them, and I although became sure that the Assad sect, despite all what they have done over many years of training and arming their men and making them control the centers of power in Syria, remained weak and stupid, and the real enemy that defeated and oppressed my Sunni Muslim People in Syria, it was their fear, their division and their weakness. These cowards only took advantage of this situation and betrayed us. Moreover, what made me laugh and increased my pleasure at that time was what I saw of the expressions of discontent, anger and envy that appeared on the faces of all the Nusayris officers who attended the meeting, after they heard about my honor, and their spiteful whispers that continued for some time after the meeting.

On a hot summer day in the month June of the year /2000/, while I was sitting in my family's home in Homs and watching the international news in English on one of the western channels, the TV broadcast was suddenly interrupted, and they reported breaking news in red, but when I read the news, I couldn't believe my eyes, and I thought my English might have betrayed me so I might have translated and understand wrongly, the news was talking about the death of Syria's tyrant Hafez al-Assad!!!!!

Then, I changed the channel to Syrian channels quickly, but I found them continuing their regular programs, so my surprise increased, what is that!? Is it wrong !? but this western channel is a global news agency and it is famous and known by honesty and accuracy in its news, and it was still confirming the news and talking about the history and crimes of the deceased. But, after waiting about half an hour I was constantly moving between Arab channels, suddenly, Syrian channels stopped broadcasting regular programs, and put classical sad music then it began to broadcast the recitation of verses from the Quran. The situation became very clear, the news is true, but they were postponing the announcement. At this moment, I don't think there is enough description of the mixture of feelings I felt, Oh My God finally ... the criminal died! The unjust died! The head and leader of the tyrants died !? who ordered to kill, cut, displace and rape my people and my country, is dead!?

Since I became aware of this world, and as a result of what I saw from sadness and oppression on the faces of most people around me, I prayed and asked Allah in every prayer to save people from this human demon, especially after I became an employee with them in the regime, and I became to see from within how much evil it is.

I've been waiting for this moment and dreaming about it all my life, I thought that the people, especially the majority

Sunni Muslims of the people, will rise up, after the snake's head was cut, and that a revolution will happen all over Syria, so that the people regain their freedom and their natural right to govern their country, and to get rid of the dirty Assad sect, hold them accountable, and punish them for the harm, oppression and repression they have done to millions of people, logically, this is the right moment to achieve the right and justice.

Of course, in the first hours after this event, I and all officers and members of the security and intelligence services in Syria were summoned immediately to join to our headquarters, and a maximum-intelligence alert was declared. When the Syrian channels were broadcasting the funeral of the tyrant, we were conducting intelligence patrols which they made us do, and during our wandered among the people in Hama, I was saying to myself as I look at the kids on the streets of this city, it is time for just retribution, it's time to take revenge from who slaughtered your fathers and your families, and punish those who did this to them. At any moment, I expected to hear the news of the popular revolution that I expected from our people, but what happened next was more amazing to me, and showed me a new reality that I never expected, although I heard with my ear whispers of cursing, abuse, invocation, and wish hell to the deceased Hafez al-Assad, among people everywhere, after confirming the news of his death, except the members of his sect of Nusayris of course, those who were astonished, terrified, and crying so badly, and their faces and actions showed that they were expecting as I had expected, that their end will be soon after Hafez al-Assad's death, despite all this the eldest child of the dead devil was brought, he is called

Bashar al-Assad, who the features of idiocy and stupidity always appeared on his face, and in full rudeness, all Syrian laws and the content of the country's constitution have been changed within minutes, like a black comedy play, and he was appointed as a successor to his tyrant father, this seemed like a gratitude for what he did of shameful crimes.

Despite everything, the continuation of the rule of the criminal sect was declared, while the repressed, aggrieved and oppressed people were watching, hearing and applauding the new tyrant, even though the blood of tens of thousands of their sons, those slaughtered by these criminals, had not dried up yet, and tens of thousands are still bleeding in the dark basements of political prisons (the places where innocent opponents are put in and tortured by the Assad regime), where the father of this new criminal put them, then, I realized regrettably that I was and still alone in what I did, and in what I was going to do, and unfortunately that dreaded tyrant before he died, he has succeeded in killing everything in the hearts of the people !!

The difficult years

After the new criminal Bashar al-Assad came to power and to lead the repressive regime in Syria, and despite rumors that were deliberately spread by all security and intelligence services in front of world, Arab and internal public opinion, which revolves around pink dreams, that the new president will gradually alleviate the approach of repression, persecution and dictatorship, that his father established, followed and strengthened in Syria, but I had an inner certainty, perhaps because I know much more of the hidden and secret details of things and the way of thinking of this ruling Nusayri sect and its leaders, that the conditions are almost impossible to change as long as the entire system and its services still exist, this is what I have always said to my friends and my people in Homs and Hama, when they were asking me about my expectations for Syria's future under Bashar, because I am a specialist in intelligence and political work.

At that time everyone around me knew, since his unlawfully inauguration in Syria, that I was never optimistic, about a better future in his era, and I shortened my opinion to those who asked in a phrase: "what was built on people's suffering and their oppression, it is better when the fire eats it", and what is built on wrong basis is wrong, especially that I was seeing and hearing every day during my work in the military intelligence branch in Hama the sarcastic comments which the officers and leaders of the branch made, about the rumors that were circulating among citizens about the coming changes for the better in Syria, and the reassurance, confidence and tranquility were apparent on the faces of small and large intelligence criminals, all of that never augur well. And really, in the years after Bashar took the rule, nothing has changed in the nature of my work, or the work of the Military Intelligence Branch in Hama in general, moreover, in the era of the small criminal (Bashar), the Syrian security and intelligence services began to monitor and follow new groups of innocent citizens, then they arrested them, like: human rights groups, the Damascus declaration group, the National democratic grouping, and other small new political groups and groupings which thought that the situation in Syria has changed, for me, I have continued my usual secret and public works despite the despair and frustration that I had after seeing the lack of reaction and lack of resistance among the Syrian people, while they see their country and their freedom being inherited among their enemies.

At the beginning of /2003/, Something happened that changed my situation and my life, as the Syrian regime redistributed the officers and leaders of the Syrian intelligence services, and as a result of the redistribution, Colonel Muhammad al-Sha'ar was promoted to brigadier general, then he was transferred from the Hama branch, and appointed as head of the Military Intelligence Branch in Tartus. At that time, all the officers of the branch expected that I would ask for my transfer with him because they thought I had been working for the past years for him, and he summoned me to his office before leaving for his new job because he also thought I would ask him to take me with him, but they all did not know that I have built relationships of mutual trust and cooperate for good with a large number of honest intellectuals in the city of Hama over the years, in addition, I have a network of relationships and information which always has been helping me to help a lot of citizens in different fields, and I will not give up all this easily, because I got it as a result of my efforts and me risking my life for ten years.

When the Brigadier General (al-Sha'ar) knew that I did not want to go with him to the branch of Tartus, he warned me of treachery, harm and conspiracies of all officers, he was sure that it would be directed against me in the future, and he recommended me to be very cautious from that, I thanked him for this interest, while being surprised in myself from this behavior from an officer known for his cruelty, selfishness and lack of interest in anyone !!

Among the movements that happened in the leadership of the intelligence services, a new colonel was brought to the Military Intelligence Branch in Hama, and he was chosen as the leader of the branch, he is Colonel Mohammad Ahmad Mufleh, he was supposed to be a Muslim man from the Sunni majority, and his origins go back to Bedouin clans that live in a village called /Al-mahajja /, it is one of the villages of Daraa, but the words of this officer, since the first word I heard from him in his first meeting with the officers, then the many criminal acts that he did later, it proved to me and to everyone that he is a human demon, and a real criminal, he only worships his own benefit and greed, and he doesn't give any value to religion or morality, he is more evil even than Assad's sect.

Although the Colonel Mufleh was, as was confirmed by everyone who knew him previously or worked with him in the intelligence branches where he worked, a cheap, marginalized and humiliated officer with no powers, and he was subjected to daily insults and abuses by his leadership and higher-ranking Nusayri officers, but the begging and mediating to one of the most important traitors of the people and the Sunni majority, who participated in the crimes of al-Assad's father and son, he is Farouk al-Sharaa, who is a relative of Colonel Mufleh, at that time he was the Vice-President (of course, it is an imaginary position only to the media, and no real powers were given to him like all other Sunni officials in the both Assad regimes, the father's and the son's), this relationship made Mohammad Mufleh finally getting the job as the leader of the military intelligence branch in Hama, which was for him the maximum of his hopes and dreams. He intended to preserve it by any way, even if this mean is the blood and souls of the innocent people of his religion, his nation, his sect and his homeland. In fact, that was what he did later throughout his work as head of this branch, and from the earliest years of his leadership, it seemed clear to everyone that his plan of all his work, and what he made the Military Intelligence Branch work for, is to reach two goals:

- The first: raising money through any way possible no matter how dirty it is, like: establishing partnerships with drug traffickers, arms dealers, smugglers of goods, human traffickers, people who are working in prostitution, and white slave traders, even with embezzlers, bribers and thieves he have established friendships, partnerships and friendly relations, this partnerships were based on the principle of Mufleh providing them with protection, legal cover and intelligence tolerance about them and their dirty deeds, for money and very large gains they give to this criminal in various ways and forms. And because of these agreements and their results, the cars which were loaded with precious gifts and money were arriving and handed to Colonel Mohammad al-Mufleh at the branch headquarters and at his house every day, at day and night, throughout his working in Hama.

- The second goal: It was making the intelligence leaders satisfied with him in any way, no matter how dirty or criminal, in addition to proving his absolute loyalty to the Assad regime, and denying any doubts about this loyalty because of his belonging to the majority of Sunnis, in order to be able to maintain his existence, his gains, and to remain in his position as Head of the Military Intelligence Branch in Hama, for someone without conscience like Mufleh it was the easiest and fastest way to achieve this goal, it is giving human sacrifices from the weak, honorable, the poor, and those who have nothing to give, from the natives of Hama, to the altar of the Assad regime, especially, of course, from Sunni Muslims until the Assad community being well satisfied.

During the years when Mufleh was the leader and manager of the branch, who was promoted to brigadier general, I was seeing the branch filled with poor innocent and honorable people who were dragged from Hama, as a result of dirty reporting that corruption mafias were fabricating about them, to remove them from their corruption's and interests' way. And after the people in Hama were under the oppression and persecution from the regime and the Assad sect for decades, in the era of Brigadier General Mufleh injustice and persecution of new mafias of corruption economically and financially were added to the people's misery.

After a short period of time, the members and the officers of the Hama branch along with them the corrupt persons in Hama city and the government departments whom I have been fighting against for many years and always standing in the their way, they felt that finally the time to take revenge on me and remove me away from their path, had come, and that my frontline became exposed after the removal of the protection that the Brigadier General al-Sha`ar was offering to me – and I was considering it a help and blessing from God-, and that it became possible to get rid of me. Immediately, they began forming alliances and holding meetings to agree on how to do it, and then as they didn't found any charge or financial suspicion going on around me, which is usually available and applied to most other intelligence officers, then they tried to fabricate charges against me of religious fanaticism, and that I intend to persecuting non-Muslim citizens of other sects in my work.

So they prepared a huge file against me, and provided it with numerous testimonies from corrupt officials, whom I had try during my working years to stop their corruption and hold them accountable, and they submitted this file to the head of the branch, with the support of branch officers and senior mafia leaders whom I mentioned earlier, but Allah Almighty with His generosity and mercy made one of the Nusayris member, his name is Jamal, whom I previously had provided with assistance that saved him from a bad situation (I did this as part of my plan to get closer to the officers and get information from them), he suddenly decided after he knew about the plot against me (and he was hesitant whether he would share it or not) to reveal the whole subject, as I was surprised how he told me the details of what was lurked against me secretly. Then he asked to meet the branch head Mufleh, and explained that what happened was fabricated, and a plot to get rid of me. And because of his testimony, this first attempt was stopped, and I survived, thanks to God.

But after this incident, the Brigadier General Mufleh realized that his partners in filth would never be happy because of my existence, and because of his baseness, he basically didn't need any charge or excuse to remove me from their way, he was the last one who care about the law. Also, the reports and intelligence topics, that I submitted to the branch, were not the type he liked or cared about, especially that I was fighting one of the most important sources of his illicit livelihood.

Based on all of that, he started harming and surrounding me immediately, as he suddenly issued an order, without reason to move me from the Economic Office to the Office of Intelligence Studies in the branch, furthermore, he has become periodically issuing decisions that achieve evil desires which the Nusayri officers had dreamed of implementing against me long ago, and I became under their constant surveillance. Based on their proposals Mufleh began to move me between the sections and offices in the branch, to manipulate my nerves psychologically then he began to prevent me from working completely and froze my actions by keeping me in the Branch, he found in what he was doing with me an opportunity for new gains, by bargaining about it with those who hate me inside and outside the branch, and a good way to prove his loyalty and blind obedience to the al-Assad sect, as he demonstrated to them that he never cares for the members of his sect, whom I represented as one of them.

During this period, I have lived very difficult and bad years, especially that the accursed Mufleh was almost every month, for very trivial reasons, putting me in the dark, isolated underground prison at the branch, for periods ranging from one to two weeks. I had children, so my work and its very bad conditions, as well as my frequent absences from my children, became very difficult to bear. During these black years of my life, I had been exposed to another serious attempt to get rid of me permanently, but this time the aim was to obtain an order by the Assad regime to execute me completely. This attempt had a very strange and amazing story!!

One time, I was serving one of the prison sentences which the head of the branch "Mufleh" had ordered to enforce at me under the pretext of being a little late for work, at this time I was amazed and surprised because my sentence in prison was extended until I reached sixteen days in it. And when I finally came out, and after some days, when a Nussayri officer asked me to talk with me privately, this person is named Basel Shahoud, /he is from a small Nusayri village in the countryside of Homs, its name is Tarin Village/, his face showed that he was very hesitant and fearful, and when I agreed, he asked me: do you know what happened in the branch while you were in prison?

I replied: No of course, how will I know anything while I am in prison, isolated from the outside world and underground!?

He said: Do you swear on that!?

I replied: Yes.

Then he began to tell me that while I was in prison, one of the corrupt officers in the military intelligence branch in Hama, -his name is Colonel Abdul Hamid, who was a dirty officer, addicted to alcohol and going to brothels- had agreed with one of the famous pimps in the city of Hama, named Izz al-Din, who was working in the trade and facilitation of prostitution for high-level officials, and several times I had disrupted his suspicious works, with him were also another group of people who resemble him and belong to the same decadent level, they all agreed to direct a fatal hit against me this time, when they finished the file that they all prepared against me, by which they accused me that I am against the state, thus, Colonel Abdul Hamid literally promised them that he would "send me behind the sun". In Syria, this term means: being arrested for ever or immediate execution. According to what the officer Basel told me, they worked secretly and intensively when I was in prison, and they brought for that so many witnesses from my enemies, to fabricate, against me, various charges such as sectarianism and other deadly charges in the law of the Assad regime. The one who was directly supervising the investigation against me, is another evil and hateful Nusayri officer named Yassin Muhammad from a Nusayri village named Alsawmaa, one of Masyaf's villages in Syria.

Basel continued his story, that when they finished the file, and they were ready to send it to the capital Damascus to eliminate me, something very strange happened, that in the night when they were supposed to send the file in the morning, the central heating system was damaged so that the hot water flowed all night towards the office, then, it flowed into the drawer where the file prepared against me was, so it was damaged completely. In the next morning, Colonel Abdul Hamid and officer Yassin went mad when they knew this, and began accusing treason to each other and to the others participants in the plot, then they came to think that one of them told me about it while I was inside the prison, then I sent someone who opened the heating water on the file to deliberately damage it.

Thereupon, Basel told me that they decided to cancel the plan for now, because they did not like to call the witnesses and the participants in the plot back to the branch and take their statements again, because they will become mockery for everyone, and discredit their own reputation and that of the whole branch, also then everyone will know that they couldn't take care of the file, and that they didn't back it up either. When Basel finished telling me this, as much as I was angry at the treachery and evil that these criminals I work among have and use, the more I praised Allah - the Almighty - and thanked him a lot, and I was so grateful because I considered that he made that water like a soldier of His army which saved me and failed the unjust people and made them shocked.

This was not the end of the story, after a short period of time, two amazing things also happened, First, a sharp disagreement happened between Colonel Abdul Hamid and Brigadier-General Mufleh on personal ambitions, as a result, Colonel Abdul Hamid was fired and accused of fraud, then he became a wanted fugitive to the Assad regime. As for the officer Yassin Muhammad, he was injured during a very serious road accident while driving a motorcycle, and both hands were broken which he had previously used in an attempt to harm me, so glory to Allah the Avenger, the Mighty of the heavens and the earth.

One of the most important heinous crimes committed by Brigadier General Mufleh, during my time in the branch, is the fabrication of the case /Jund al-Sham/; so, what is this case!?

The years that were passing at that time were the first years of the internet in Syria, the young people and students in schools and universities found in it what they thought to be areas of freedom of expression, and they were beginning to learn how to use websites and blogs, and how they communicate through it, these simple people did not know that a criminal system that is professional in methods of repression, like the Assad regime, will only allow them to acquire and use these technologies after making sure that he has the equipment, tools and means to monitor and spy on them. So, as a result to what I just explained, the new arrests that were carried out by the intelligence services in Syria were not as those in the past that were because of a talk or an act of one of the citizens, rather, blogging or posting on the internet things that criticize a regime official or law, have become a new reason for the prosecution and detention of a number of citizens in general, and especially young people, who were the most using group of the internet at the time.

In 2007, after a number of arrests of a group of young students from Hama by the military intelligence branch in Hama, because of charges of this type, the Brigadier General, Mufleh, had a satanic idea that he considered a way to bring himself closer to the leaders of the Assad regime and make them satisfied about him and about his criminal level, doing so, he will hold higher positions in the future; this idea was to create a dangerous new imaginary enemy of the Assad regime, so that he can represents the great hero who discovered this danger, and destroyed it in front of this regime, how did that happen !?

Before a period of time, Islamic strict groups Appeared in Lebanon, a country neighboring Syria, its name was / Jund al-Sham /, and there was a huge media outcry at the time because of the clash of these groups with the Lebanese army. Brigadier General Mufleh found this an opportunity for him, when he gave orders to impose confessions on some young university students from Hama, who were arrested for minor online activities, that they are members of Jund al-Sham, and everyone in Syria knows that the torture in the security and intelligence prisons continues until the accused dies, or confesses to whatever the interrogator wants, and the subject has been fabricated in an elaborate manner by Mufleh and his associates in the branch about the regimentation, members, activities, etc.

This information was sent to the maniac President Bashar al-Assad the Syrian president in Damascus at the time, and they obtained a decision from him allowing the Military Intelligence Branch in Hama to deal with citizens in any way and as they want, to investigate in this subject, at that time we all in the branch knew that the whole subject was fabricated. Then, and for nearly two years, the Brigadier General Mufleh has launched a campaign of arrests of individuals, and raids on houses; the campaign was continuous and intense, and he recruited for it all the officers of the branch, its workers, its mechanisms, its possibilities, and its detachments; during this campaign, he didn't leave any family in Hama or its villages without arresting a number of their young sons, whom all were from Sunni Muslims exclusively as usual. Throughout two full years, the branch cells, basements and offices were full of young people detained in day and night, and Mufleh was wandering around them every day, and he personally supervised the torture, burning, cutting, and electrocuting of the detainees. The cries of pain and torment were filling the branch; the pain was filling my heart, when I saw these young people whose most of them were studying specializations in Syrian universities such as engineering, pharmacy and medicine.

Mufleh's instructions to the investigators in the branch were clear, specific and public, that is to continue the torture to death, or to admit of what he wants and needs to complete his fabricated story about Jund al-Sham; and I have heard from interrogators several times about Mufleh's direct orders, when they tell him that the arrested young man knows nothing and does not admit anything, the answer of Muflih always was .. kill him .. if he did not confess to anything, so they continue to torture him until he dies. Really, there were deaths every period among these weak and poor people; although the Nusayri officers of the branch were pleased with what the criminal Mufleh was doing for their regime, but they could not hide their surprise from the amount of evil and the criminal mind that this devil have, and the amount of fabrication which the files of detainees were made from, to prove his lie that he invented and called it Jund al-Sham.

I remember that at the end of this subject, after the branch raided a house where a group of unarmed young civilians were present, in the Aleppo Road neighborhood in Hama, at that time, an innocent child was killed, he was present by chance with his father in that house, where during the raid, members of the branch opened fire on him by order of Brigadier General Mufleh, when his father attempted to exit surrendering with his child from home. The child's presence in this house was evidence of innocence and peacefulness of those who were in it. Thereafter, Mufleh brought a large quantity of weapons, machine guns, explosives and bombs from the armories in the branch, and brought it to the house where the raid took place; after putting it in the house, some dust and sand were sprayed on the weapons to make them look used, then he invited the Al Jazeera Arabic news station to film the event and the house, under the title "Arrest of a dangerous armed gang of Jund al-Sham in a house that was a den of them", and I was a witness to that and I saw the details by myself, as most of the other officers of branch saw.

By the year 2009, I had been working in the Military Intelligence administration in Syria among these criminal enemies for fifteen years, I had arrived to a state of extreme physical and intellectual fatigue, fifteen years and I live among the most evil people and despicable criminals, I was surrounded by people that between them and me there is a common hatred, and with all what disagrees with my religion, moral and customs, I see the crimes, injustice, theft, cheating, prostitution, alcoholics and all kinds of shameful and dirty things around me, moreover, I had to live with the doers and addicts of these things, long years went from my age, and I spent my youth sleeping among my enemies, expecting in any sound or movement from them that they will betray me, every time I allowed one of the oppressed wanted persons to escape, or leaked information to anyone, or destroyed the information inside the files of branch, I was at risk of being arrested and subjected to the worst forms of torture, or being executed immediately.

Although I had lost, in the time when the criminal brigadier general Mufleh was the leader of the branch, a lot of my former ability to move freely, and I was always under surveillance, but I was able every period of time, thanks to Allah, until the last moments I spent in this branch, to save an innocent person from time to time, but this year I reached the point that I was feeling very upset, and I couldn't bear this life anymore, so I made the decision, that I must get myself out of this work and of this decadent place in whatever way, despite the opposition of many honest friends in making this decision, those who followed, watched, know and heard what I had been doing with the people of their city over the years, they tried to persuade me repeatedly to reverse my decision, and reminded me that I was a small space of hope and a glimmer of light for many people in Hama, and others of my acquaintances in Homs and Hama were deeply amazed at my decision to leave wide powers and legal immunity that I have wherever I go in Syria, because I'm an intelligence officer, but I answered them by the words of Allah in his book the Holy Quran {Allah never order or force any soul except what it can do or bare}, and now I have children, they must have rights from my time, life and a share of my thinking.

Implementing my decision of leaving the Syrian Intelligence Services was not easy at all, as most Syrians know, no officer or employee was allowed to leave this work except in very special cases, so this took me intense efforts, repeated requests, persistence and urgency for a whole year. During this period, I was subjected to various pressures and threats to make me retract the requests I made to leave or change my job. After all of this, and after an interview, I was summoned to it, with one of the top security and intelligence leaders in Syria, one of the founders of this system, and he is also an adviser to both the al-Assad father and the son, he is the Nusayri Major General Ali Younes (just mentioning his name was enough to cause panic even for the leaders and officers of the intelligence branches in Syria), there was a very long debate and discussion between me and him, during it, he tried to encourage me sometimes and at other times to intimidate me to retract my decision. When he realized the intensity of my insistence on my request, he told me that he had no authority to laid me off from my work because I'm an old warrant officer with many years of intelligence field work experience, I became an expert in military intelligence work, and I have a medal of appreciation in this field, he told me that if I persist, he can only move me to easier work in the regular army outside the Military Intelligence administration if I want, I immediately agreed, of course, my most important goal was salvation from the Military Intelligence administration.

In the early days of 2010, I was transferred to the Department of Military Engineers of the Syrian Army.

When I finally got out safely from the gates of the Military Intelligence Branch in Hama, after about seventeen years I spent in the intelligence service, sixteen years of it in this accursed branch, there were no words that could describe my beautiful feeling and my unlimited happiness, and I was in that moment about to kneel on earth (like Muslims always do when they want to thank or pray to Allah) during my exit from the main gate of the branch, but I was knowing how dangerous this behavior will be if they notice me, and I came out while I was thanking Allah with all my heart for the blessings, that I got out safely from this place, and after having achieved a good part of my goals, which I entered this work many years ago to implement it.

I succeeded -because of Allah's blessing and helping- to get in this dirty Intelligence system den, and got out, when I wanted that, even though I didn't know, during every day of these long years, if I would be able to go home in that day or not.

So, I said gratefully: "Praise and Thanks be to Allah always and forever".

Notice: I want to mention at the end of this chapter, and in order to be a witness against criminals, the names of officers who participated in harming people in the Hama Military Intelligence Branch, and their names were not mentioned, such as:

- Captain Ghassan Jawad
- Major Firas Al-Asaad
- Colonel Adel Mustafa
- Colonel Haitham Nader (he is living nowadays in the United States)
- Major Mohamed Darwish
- Colonel Abdul Hamid Idris
- Colonel Abdul Hamid Al-Harraq
- Major General Hasan Khallouf.

We hope that all criminals in Syria will be judged with fair trials.

Two years in the army
...and the blessed Syrian revolution

The first year which I spent in the Syrian army was in the military center devoted to the maintenance of heavy vehicles near my city Homs. And my work there for me was like a recovery and I considered it a rest period after long exhausting years in Military Intelligence. Although most of the squalor and problems in the intelligence system, such as sectarianism, widespread corruption, bribery, favoritism and others, exist also in the army ;but their amount and magnitude, and the struggle for them here was much simpler and on lower level. The most important of all is that the army had a good percentage of Sunni Muslim officers, individuals, and recruits, and from almost all the Syrian regions. Therefore, my presence and work in the army was natural and acceptable to others, and not strange and anomalous, as it was in the Intelligence administration. Although it is never easy for any person to adapt to changing the place and nature of his work after many years spent in the first work, I quickly accepted everything, and everything went easy with God's helping.

On March 15th, 2011, while I was sitting at my house watching TV, I was amazed by the scene of the first small demonstration against the Syrian regime, which took place in one of Damascus' Bazaars in Syria. One of the satellite channels (Orient News) was broadcasting video clips of this demonstration. I do not think that anyone in the world was happier than me in those moments, in which I could see my dream and my father's dream - may God have mercy on his soul - and the dream of most of the people I knew around me throughout my life, finally beginning to become true. I used to see the people, who for decades remained suffering their humiliation and oppression while they were silent as the death, finally returning to life again. Yes, I was finally seeing the target of my sacrifices, and what I and many others had sacrificed for previously throughout our life, all of It finally became valuable.

During the following months, the events accelerated, and the flame of demonstrations moved from one place to another. Until they started in my city Homs, which later became the capital and center of this revolution. With God's helping, I participated in all first demonstrations against the Assad regime, which were occurring in Homs every week, going out from the mosques. The worshipers were demonstrating after they leave Friday prayers in those mosques.

I was always participating in the demonstrations, despite extreme danger and the bad consequences if the regime forces caught me compared to the other participants. This is because I am a military person, not a civilian like others. This means that the punishment in this case for me, according to the laws of the regime, is immediate field execution, but God saved me. After that, the Assad regime began punishing the city by cutting off water, electricity, communications and heating fuel for all the revolutionary neighborhoods, including of course my home. We had been without these requirements for a long time, and our conditions as a result - and with us all the people around us - became very difficult.

During the same period, and due to the events at that time, the Nusayris who worked with us in the army lost their minds. And They became more hostile, sectarian and fierce towards us. We were seeing them every day, after they finish working with us, being ordered and meeting together with the directives of the intelligence branches, and usually come with them also all the men in the Nusayri villages which surround Homs. They were supplied with weapons and transported in buses in large numbers to the city to participate with the intelligence services in the crimes that the regime had begun to commit daily in Homs to put down the revolution. They were indiscriminately killing and slaughtering innocents barbarically in the city's neighborhoods, kidnapping and raping women, looting and then burning houses. Because of this, the revolutionaries began to have to defend themselves and their families with their light weapons, and honorable army personnel began to defect from the regime and formed an armed resistance to defend the innocents.

Therefore, I made my decision immediately - without hesitation - to defect from the regime and participate in protecting the people. This is what I've been waiting for all my life. I started communicating with revolutionary groups in the neighborhoods around my house and gathering information about them in order to find the right group for me to join. I had known that there is a group of revolutionaries with a very good reputation and its leader is loved by people and known for his high morals. The group was named after its leader /Abu Asaad Group/. They were centered in Al-Bayyada neighborhood in Homs city. Earlier, I had leaked intelligence and military information to them which I obtained through my work in the army about the existence of regime spies among a group of revolutionaries (which was stationed in the village of Za`farana), and about the regime's intention to raid that group at their base. My information has saved the lives of the members of the Za`farana group. Therefore, Abo Asaad, the leader of the Bayyadah Group, thanked me very much for this when I first met him. He also begged me at that time to keep leaking in a secret way military and intelligence information to them while I was still working. He said that this would be more beneficial and most important for them than leaving my work and joining them completely and openly, because they currently have enough numbers of fighters and leaders. Indeed, we agreed to this and I became a defector from the regime, and I was working and helping for the benefit of the revolution and the revolutionaries officially, but in secret.

In the early morning of a cold winter day of the third month March of 2012, at that time an almost complete month had passed while we were living without water, electricity or heating, and while we were having breakfast my family and I, at our house in the al-Ta'menat neighborhood in Homs (It is a part of the famous neighborhood al-khalidiya), during that the Assad regime bombed my house and all the homes of the neighborhood we live in with various types of missiles after its siege, as part of the regime's plan that it had been implementing by destroying the neighborhoods from which demonstrations against them came. The sound of explosions and screams of pain and panic around us, started and intensified without warning. The bodies of innocents and bloods filled the streets of the neighborhood. But with the help of God I succeeded in taking my family out under snipers' fire, and between the explosions of the shells. I managed to smuggle them from the siege imposed on the neighborhood. I came out with them with difficulty, with the help of some of the revolutionaries from the group I work with, who were accidentally present in the neighborhood as a result of their attempts to rescue some of the innocent children injured in it. My family and I were among the few families who were able to escape under the fire of the Assad regime in that day, due to the deadly danger of trying to leave, so that most families failed to do so. But our going out was only with our clothes on. On that day, we lost all the money, official papers, clothes, and personal belongings we had, as we left them all in the house that the Assad regime (supervised by Air Force Intelligence branch in Homs) in the days following that day, bombed, looted and then burned, along with all the other houses of the neighborhood.

The detention
... Six months of torture and the terrible Tadmur Prison in Palmyra

About two months later, exactly in the fifth month of 2012, after my house and its furniture were destroyed, and my children and I became homeless, temporarily living as guests in our relatives' homes, I decided to move to a new stage. I no longer tolerated my current situation and to just work secretly with the revolution, while I am obliged to remain in the army while working with these criminals. They were publicly proud every day and in front of us of the crimes they commit against us and our city of Homs. My presence with them, despite its usefulness to the men of the revolution, became illogical in my view. In the period before, I have been preparing to carry out a major collective defection from the army, and have prepared a number of personnel, recruits and officers who are ready for this idea. We all agreed that I would secure cars through the group of revolutionaries with whom I work to transport everyone at the agreed ache-hour. I also transported and stockpiled weapons and ammunition from army depots to my office under the pretext of increased cautiousness and protection because of the revolution, while our real goal was to bring these weapons with us to the revolutionaries during our defection and escape from the army.

On May 11th, 2012, one of the Sunni officers who worked with us provoked the Nusayri soldiers. So, and as a result of the plan that the Assad regime started to implement a while ago, by eliminating all Sunni officers and officials in all sectors of the Syrian army, because it was fearing that they and the people would turn against it, forces of the military intelligence branch of Homs arrested me at that morning with group of soldiers and recruits. This was happening even though I had already prepared myself for this possibility. I had intended in this case to resist with my weapon and not surrender to them. However, they used a trick by assuring me that they just wanted to consult me about an issue. I was then taken to Military Intelligence Detachment in the village of Al-Mushrifah, in Homs countryside, and then transferred to the headquarters of the Military Intelligence Branch in Homs, and I was placed in the branch prison.

In fact, it is very difficult to describe to the reader the true degree of the bad conditions in the Syrian Intelligence detention centers, and the amount of very poor conditions in which the detainees are placed. I think these places are the closest they can be to a picture that a man's mind imagines about hell. Although I had spent a large part of my life in the Syrian intelligence service, and I had previous information and observations about the dungeons used by this regime, and even that - as I mentioned earlier - I was imprisoned several times in the same way before, but after the Syrian revolution, everything I knew differed. Things got a lot worse. The numbers of detainees increased dramatically, as did brutality in dealing with them, and powers were given to torturers to kill any detainee at any moment.

From the first moment in which a detainee enters the political prison, he feels that he has become out of the world and time. He feels like he's become in a world of endless nightmares. The first thing that he is forced to do is to strip himself completely from his clothes in front of others (naked and afraid like the day his mother gave birth to him), as if he would be born again in this black underworld, the world of prisons. For a society that maintains traditions, religion, and customs, such as ours, it is a severe form of humiliation and subjugation. The man in our society suffers when others see him naked. After that, the torturers start emptying their sectarian and criminal filth with whips, sticks, and cuffs on each detainee by starting to hitting them, and this is accompanied by a torrent of dirty and disgusting words that come out of the mouths of these torturers as insults, debasements, and blasphemous words with insulting all sanctities of all religions in the world. They pour all of this on the detainee.

The hitting and beating that I saw were not only done by the torturers in the detention places during the period of the Syrian revolution with the aim of torture only, but it was clear that it was intended to kill or at least cause the detainee to have permanent fractures in his body. After all that, and when the torturers get tired or bored, they throw the victim naked and completely covered with his blood over the other detainees' piles inside the cells. In these cells, for me, the real torture was the air ... yes the oxygen, as breathing the air in this place was the most difficult thing for me, even though the other causes that caused pain and suffering for me and everyone are very many. There was no water for the detainees, but only leaking dirty water from the often-missing baths, and the little food which we get was intentionally stinky, rotten and contaminated with various types of dirt. Going to the toilet to urinate or defecate was needing a very long waiting, and it finally took place and was done in a dirty place that made the detainees' bodies and limbs contaminate more and more with human excrement. In the absence of water and soap, this garbage remained attached to everyone, and even the scene that I was seeing (and the rest of the detainees) was torture itself. We used to see people of all ages and sizes wherever we looked in the cell's darkness, including the elderly, children, the injured and the dying persons, all of them were tightly crammed in very narrow places, and their bodies and the rest of their torn clothes were contaminated with dry blood, pus and dirt.

The scabies and pediculosis, which immediately affected any new detainee as a result of compulsory attachment to the bodies of others afflicted with these lesions, make all of them, day and night, permanently suffering of bouts of itching and hysterical scratching. And whenever you look at the prisoners' faces, you see some of them appearing shocked, stunned, distracted, absent-minded, some of the others cry, and a lot of them suffer or they feel that they will lose their brains' balance and the beginnings of madness appear on them. All of that is accompanied by the cries of pain, groaning and wailing which never stop in this place.

I remember well all the very sad scenes that I saw inside the darkness of political prisons, which are more like graves. I do not forget when I saw a man who was close to ninety years old sitting between the feet of prisoners and nearly dying with his head hanging on his chest, and when I tried to help him and give him some water He told me with great sadness and pain that the criminal Assad regime arrested him twice, although he is old, and each time they told him that the reason for his imprisonment was the resemblance of his name to another person, but that happens after he had experienced a lot of torture, humiliation, and pain every time!

Also, I remember a young man under the age of twenty years who was among the prisoners, with a medical device hanging between his feet that is used to empty body fluids when the situation of the patient is so bad that he is unable to urinate! And every day, especially at night, we clearly heard the screams, wailing, and crying of women and children from the adjacent prison sections in the intelligence center in Homs, and there was also an old man with us who always cried, and he did not stop crying and said that he did not cry because of his wounds and pain, even though they are many, Rather, he is crying because when the regime's soldiers arrested him, they took his wife and daughters with him and put them in another place to prepare them to be raped, and he no longer knows anything about their fate! I always asked myself whenever I saw such cases, what makes the Assad regime and its demons arrest such sick and weak people !? And what is the harm that these people can do that made the regime fear them and imprison them !? Or is the Assad regime filthy, oppressive, and mean to the point that it does not resemble humans or animals !?

However, as I mentioned earlier, in addition to all this suffering, I complained a lot from difficulty of breathing. The little air in our underground dungeon was rotten, stubborn, and full of blood odors with feces, mold, and human sweat scents emitted from dirty bodies. In general, the air was a mixture of what the human soul hates and is disgusted by. I remained in the first two months of my detention having asthma-like suffocation cases. Because of its intensity, I thought every time that it would be the way God chose for me to leave the world. I remained from the first day of my detention and imprisonment into the cell for seventeen days without being able to defecate, and I did not eat every day more than a small rotten crumb. At the end of these days, I reached a severe state of weakness, disease and pain. I also sometimes could not move at all.

At this time, when I reached this condition, the Assad regime investigators in the Military Intelligence Branch in Homs began interrogating me. They had to drag me on the floor or carry me every time to be able to get me to the torture and interrogation room. From the first interrogation session, I made it clear to the investigator that I had experience in his work, and what he would do with me, because I spent many years working in the Intelligence administration. Therefore, because of my knowledge that he will never let me and will not stop his torture for me until he receives my confessions (I was afraid because my health was so bad and maybe I will lose my consciousness during the torture and speak about a lot of the revolution secrets that I know and that may cause harm to a lot of revolutionaries so I chose to sacrifice myself), I will make for him an offer that will make him comfort and relieves and saves his time and effort. Under this offer, I will immediately sign all the charges against me, and I will confess to the acts he wants to accuse me of. The interrogator was happy with this early surrender, and he did not hesitate to direct a variety of charges against me. These charges are mocking Syrian army and intelligence forces, damaging their reputation, mocking the national economy, and making and spreading rumors that insult the regime. I confessed to all these charges as in our agreement. Despite my severe illness at that time, I once again felt the absurdity and stupidity of the Assad regime and its officers. This is because if they had known what I was and would still be doing with their system truly during the course of my work in the intelligence or army, and the amount of my cooperation and alliance with every revolutionary against them and their regime, they would have executed me immediately, and they wouldn't only stop at these simple and silly accusations against me, but God blinded their insights and eyes.

Although the investigator was pleased and satisfied with the results obtained from me, he continued for two whole weeks to torture me and interrogate me daily. His investigation with me began during that period every evening, tying my arms backwards with ropes and then hanging them while they were attached to the ceiling in a way that was intended to take off the shoulders under the pressure of the heavy weight on them. The interrogator was keeping me in this state every time until the early hours of dawn. His goal was to try to get from me, after I confessed about myself what they wanted, new confessions of names and information about any people who participated in any way in the activities of the Syrian revolution in the neighborhoods of the city of Homs. However, despite my pain and illness, I continued to deny my knowledge of any names, even though in reality I was at that time aware of everything about almost all the revolutionaries of Homs.

I felt in myself with confidence and honesty that I was fully prepared to die before I cause any harm to any of the heroes who revolted against these oppressors. At the end of two weeks of my daily torture, the interrogator stopped everything and told me that he was tired of me. After that, he asked me to sign and put my fingerprints on my previous statement and confessions. One of the things I remember in one of the interrogation sessions is that, while I was fastened in the way I mentioned earlier, the investigators brought in a young man, about eighteen years old, and put him on torture machines. Then, four of the torturers gathered to torture this poor young man, and each of them possessed a different tool that he uses to harm him. In the meantime, they told him that they would not let him until he confessed to killing anyone from the regime. The poor young man was shouting that he could not kill any living creature, but they continued to beat him until he agreed that the investigators would write whatever confessions they wanted about any crimes they wanted from him, and he would sign it immediately. Indeed, they made him sign false confessions that he had previously shot a gathering of Assad regime officers, and that he had killed four of them.

After spending about fifty-seven days in the Military Intelligence Branch prison in Homs, I was transferred to the Military Police Branch prison in the same city. However, before my final exit from the Military Intelligence branch, I saw something that I will never forget. I saw a huge truck parked in the branch square opposite the prison gate intended for the arrest of women. The backside of the truck was fully loaded with bloodstained women bags and strollers. I immediately recalled the stories of the kidnapping of women and children carried out by the Assad regime forces, in partnership with criminals who they brought from the Nusayri villages, those women and Children were kidnapped from the homes and streets of the neighborhoods that oppose the regime, and from the homes of people who participated in the demonstrations against the regime in the city of Homs, which we knew some cases and heard about others in every day since the revolution began in 2011.

After I was handed over to the Military Police branch of Homs, I was deported again at the same day after they tied me and many detainees to each other at arms and feet with metal chains. They crammed us over each other in closed trucks - that are normally used to transport livestock – and transported us to the Military Police Command in Damascus, and then to Branch 248. Branch 248 is the Military Investigation Branch of the Military Intelligence administration in Damascus, and is one of the largest and most famous centers of torture and detention in Syria since the era of the biggest criminal Hafez al-Assad. The prison of the aforementioned branch consists of a number of dark underground floors and levels. Since the detainee enters this branch until he leaves it - if he goes out - he never sees the sunlight inside it, and he does not know his day from his night. There were detainees who had not left this place for decades. In this branch, I was exposed to almost the same as what happened to me previously in the Homs branch, but the cells in Branch 248 were also more crowded than the previous branch, to the point that the miserable detainees had to organize a role between them and wait for long periods to obtain a very small area being provided by others to sit a little time between their feet. I spent about a month in the prison of this branch. One of the most painful things about me during this period was that I was almost three months gone away from my children and my family, and this took place in unusual circumstances that Syria was going through. Killing, bombing, kidnapping and many other dangers were taking place everywhere in Syria. Therefore, I did not know during this time whether my children were still alive and well or something bad happened to them, and also I knew that they also did not know anything about the condition and location of their father, in addition to being homeless as I explained earlier.

After approximately twenty-eight days in detention in Branch 248, I was transferred again in the same previous way to the Military Police Command in Damascus, and from there to the Military Police prison in Homs. There, I and many of the detainees were brought to the Military Prosecution judges in Homs, who were confirming charges about intelligence matters against everyone without any investigation or evidence. From that place, I was transferred by the judge to Tadmur Military Prison in Palmyra, this prison which all Syrians know, and also it has international reputation in being one of the worst prisons and political detention centers in the world. In this prison, many and continuous massacres and executions were committed over the years by the Assad regime to tens of thousands of innocent detainees in that place. Since childhood I have heard almost always stories of what the Assad regime is doing with detainees in this prison almost daily.

Indeed, when I was put in this prison and in the cells reserved for political detainees like me, I realized that the reputation of this place and the bad stories about it are true. God willing, I didn't just saw and was imprisoned in this place. Due to maintenance work that was taking place in our cell, I was also transferred, during that time, to areas and dungeons that had been closed since 1980, the date of the massacre carried out by the criminal Rifaat al-Assad, brother of Hafez al-Assad on, when he and his forces opened fire on the detainees at these cells and killed them all. I saw with my own eyes the traces of gunshots filling the internal walls of the cells, and there were also dry remains on the walls, which I think are remains of human limbs.

In Palmyra prison, they used to give us bitter, salty, and polluted water, and I think it was poisoned, and I am almost sure of that because the painful and terrible spasms in the stomach and intestines began to afflict me after I drank that water, and even now, although many years have passed, those still remain. Fits and pain always afflict me, and although I examined my body with several doctors and in several countries, none of them knew the reason for that!

After nearly three continuous months have passed since my detention in Tadmur Prison, and due to the severe shortage in the number of Syrian army soldiers at the time as a result of the many defections and arrests within this army, the criminal Bashar al-Assad issued a presidential pardon at the end of the eleventh month of 2012. So, I was released from Tadmur Prison in Palmyra based on that pardon, but it imposed for me a condition to return to my work and to work in the army. I finally left Tadmur Prison after a journey of torture and suffering in the regime's prisons and detention centers for a period of about six months. When I got out, my health was very bad. I lost most of my weight and turned into a pile of skin and bones. Diseases and epidemics were ravaging my body. I suffered during and after my arrest from gastrointestinal bleeding, colon spasms and gallstones. Lice and scabies also had made grooves in my skin, and this required time and effort until I recovered, thanks to God to him belong praise and thanks in any case. On my return trip to my city, my family, and my children, I was as seeing the light, the world, and the people for the first time in my life.

The second defection
the chase ... and the trip getting out of Syria

I was supposed, according to the laws of the Assad regime and the advice of most of the people around me, to return to my work in the Syrian army immediately after my release from detention. The advice of those who were detained with me, officers and military personnel, was to join my work there again for a short period only while I could get my financial salaries from the system for the six months during which I was detained, as they are usually paid to the prisoner upon his release from detention if this exit is the result of a pardon. This money would have been a good help for me and my family for the life expenses and for the costs of treatment of illnesses that I had in the prison, especially since life had become very difficult under the circumstances that Syria was going through. Then I can defect from the regime again if I insist on that. This is what others really did, whose case was similar to mine.

But I told everyone that I had deprived myself of this regime's money or anything else from it, and I would not be able to endure one more moment of being with those criminals in one place. Because of this, and after I got out of detention, I did not join as I should, and defected from the Assad regime again and forever. Of course, this meant that I had become a fugitive from my work in the army and wanted. This meant in Syria considering the state of emergency imposed by the events of the revolution, that I became, by law, condemned to death and wanted by the regime, whether alive or dead.

Therefore, I spent after this the years 2013 and 2014 as a wanted and chased fugitive. During these two years I was still in very poor health condition, without any livelihood for me and my children. I was moving secretly from place to place using disguise and hiding, and from room to room, in what remained of the destroyed neighborhoods of Homs city, which was filled with deadly danger for me, because they were all under the watching and authority of the Assad regime and its permanent control. The sudden inspection of all the houses in these neighborhoods were carried out periodically, without warning, and God saved me, by his mercy, from being arrested again several times during this period. Every time, at the last minute, I was able to escape, with my children.

In the first month of 2015, when my living conditions had become very bad and the degree of danger to my life and the lives of my family increased every day more, and I could no longer continue in this way, I decided to flee from Syria and from the Assad regime. I used intelligence papers that carry my name, because I had deceived the Military Intelligence Administration when I left work and moved to the army and kept them and did not return them to the Intelligence Administration as I was supposed to do at that time, in anticipation of any difficult future times. During my trip, I crossed more than three hundred intelligence and military checkpoints of the Assad regime. The roadblocks were spread at a rate of nearly every 200 meters along my road that I crossed from Homs to its countryside, then Hama and its countryside, then towards the city of Tabqa and its countryside, and then towards northern Syria, passing through the countryside of Raqqa and Aleppo. At each checkpoint, I was immediately exposed to arrest or killing. God was, in every new checkpoint we pass through, inspiring me through what I can cross, once I use the intelligence papers that I have, and once I hide from their eyes, and another I act like if I was an assistant to the bus driver and I am not an ordinary passenger, so as not to be subject to inspection and audit. Finally, when I arrived intact, after this dangerous journey, to the Syrian-Turkish border, I also had to walk in the darkness of a very cold winter night between snow and mud for a distance of about ten kilometers carrying my huge bag that contained everything I still owned in this world. The border area I crossed in these difficult conditions was full of trenches and barbed wires. Because of the darkness, I fell into the deep, muddy trenches several times, my clothes were torn, my body and face were injured as a result of my collision with the barbed wires and falling over them because I did not see them in the dark either.

When I finally reached the first Turkish border village, my shape and contamination with blood and mud from the top of my head to the soles of my feet were so strange and odd that it made the people of the Turkish village calling themselves out from their homes to see my shape that surprised them. Then, I realized that finally, for the first time in my life, I had fallen out of the grip of the Assad regime. After that, I remained a year working and living in Turkey, but life was very difficult for a stranger like me who did not master the language of the people of the country. Until I could afford life and feed my children, I accepted to do some jobs (in Turkey) that I never expected to do even in my worst nightmares. One of these works was, cleaning the animal pens for a salary that was barely enough for a very modest life. I always remembered how merely mentioning my name was terrifying to many corrupted ones and thieves, and respected by the honest and good people, and how I could directly get anything I wanted, then I compared it to the hardship I got. But I always go back and remind myself that all of what I did earlier aims to get God pleased with me, then for the benefit of my country and my family and my religion. This is what was giving me my patience again. After a year spent in Turkey, and because of our poor conditions, my family and I made a new journey of the kind that was called the death journey in rubber boats which are called "death boats", and that name was not without reason. They were small and simple boats of rubber, and sometimes some of them were used, old or broken. They were intended for a small number of people only, but the smugglers used to put more than fifty people in them, including children, women and old people, until you see that the boat almost sinks before it moves! The smugglers used to throw the afflicted and fleeing Syrian families in these boats over each other, and the time was often after midnight and during winter and storms, then they would order anyone in the boat who had no experience in sailing to set off towards the middle of the sea and towards the Greek islands, and the sounds of travelers, especially children and women, cry loudly and scream from fear, and they begin to pray to God to save them! Some of the passengers would reach the other shore, while most of those poor people drowned and were swallowed up by the sea, perhaps to save them from their torment and homelessness! And after that terrible suffering, we reached the continent of Europe, after that we succeeded in reaching Germany, and God made us survive, thanks to him.

We survived, yes, but until the date I wrote these lines, the Syrian people are still being killed, humiliated, and displaced in all parts of the world. The Syrian revolution for which millions sacrificed everything is still going on. / That revolution of oppressed people which most of the criminals of the earth conspired against, and with them most Systems and rulers of the earth / The result of this conspiracy is: they killed more than a million Syrians, more than 15 million were displaced, millions of injured and disappeared, hundreds of thousands are still being tortured inside the prisons of the criminal Assad and his regime, and the most sad thing is that the criminal, the tyrant of Syria, is still committing crimes against Humanity every day, and the world sees and accepts that shame for many years, the criminals who supported Assad like Russia and Iran, have turned us and our children and millions like us into miserable refugees, poor, helpless, controlled by some racist employees in most cases, we do not own homes, there is no constant work, we have lost everything, except the hope that we cling to and we will also teach our children to stick to it. God's perpetual justice says, and history also says that injustice, no matter how strong it becomes, will end and destroy itself one day.

Epilogue

In my story, I adhered to the accuracy of the information as closely as possible, and as briefly as I could, because the events and details of these long years are far more than a book in its entirety. Moreover, anyone reading it may wonder why, and what is the goal now of revealing this information that only rare few people did know completely!?

In fact, many of my generation and I have always blamed the previous generations in Syria, and we censure them for their silence over the oppressors and oppression, and for not trying to resist the domination of this oppressive sect. I wanted my children and the coming generations to know through what I wrote that we were not all surrendering, and among us was someone who was standing up and silently with his own revolution. I also wanted everyone in the world to know that if he persists in trying to rely on God, and he does not let despair overcome him, then he will succeed, God willing, one day to make a difference, even if it is small.

Freedom, justice, getting rid of injustice and oppressors, equality, equal opportunities in life, work, everything, and for everyone without exception, all of these things are worth the struggle, they deserve the sacrifice, they deserve not to surrender .. they deserve the………. REVOLUTION.

With the help of God, the arabic edition of this book was done on Friday morning, February 17th, 2017.

And this english one completed on Wednesday evening, the ninth of September 2020.

All rights (of printing, publishing and distributing the book) are reserved for the author.

Basel Muhammad Rouhi Saneeb.

E-KUTUB
Publisher of publishers
No 1 in the Arab world
Registered with Companies House in England
under Number: 07513024
Email: ekutub.info@gmail.com
Website: www.e-kutub.com
Germany Office
Linden Strasse 22, Bruchweiler 55758/
Rhineland-Palatinate
UK Registered Office:
28 Lings Coppice,
London, SE21 8SY
Tel: (0044)(0)2081334132

Lightning Source UK Ltd.
Milton Keynes UK
UKHW021238130921
390500UK00013B/849